Triumphs of Faith

IN BRAZIL WITH WESLEY AND WINNIE GOULD

by

Victor Maxwell

Contents

Foreword

IN 1958 I had finished studying Portuguese in Belem, and after a period of working on the Amazon River, I was assigned by the Field Council to work in Piracuruca, first with the Sessoms and then, on their return from furlough, with the Goulds.

Wesley and Winnie Gould were great examples of senior missionaries to me, and I learned a great deal from them. Winnie made sure I was well fed and watered and that we ate healthy food and sat at the table until the teapot was empty. She was famous for her great hospitality to both missionaries and Brazilians.

One of my greatest joys was going with Wesley and Winnie in the jeep to the various preaching points in the interior; all the while Winnie was constantly prompting Wesley to slow down.

In January 1969, after my wife Marie completed language study, we set off with our baby son to Piracuruca to take over from the Goulds for a few years. We had all our possessions in the back of the Sessoms' lorry as we travelled over the red dust roads that were full of potholes. We had to stop periodically in the darkness because the lorry overheated. When we finally arrived in Piracuruca we found that the town's generator had broken down, and the place was in darkness; however, we had a warm welcome from the believers and soon learned of the high esteem in which the people of Piracuruca held Wesley and Winnie. We were thrilled at the end of our ministry there when the church called Pastor Melo.

Several years ago we revisited Brazil. Since our time there the church has had several pastors. The Lord is blessing in Piracuruca and Batalha and the churches were packed to capacity. In Piracuruca they had recently constructed a second church modelled on the first church building.

We had times of real blessing, and on our departure, the church presented us with a plaque and one for the Goulds. The exact words inscribed on the plaque summarise the thoughts of the Brazilian believers: *"The time is passing but nobody could erase from our hearts the gratitude to God and to you for the pioneering work done with so much love and kindness."*

Our prayer is that the Goulds' story will be a blessing to you.

Edmund Norwood

CHAPTER 1

Slippery and Smelly

BILLOWING CLOUDS OF red dust kicked up behind the old Chevrolet van as it trundled along the bumpy highway in Brazil's hinterland. While the blue vehicle bounced along, Wesley Gould clung tightly to the steering wheel, trying to negotiate his way around numerous potholes and avoid the eroded edges of the rough road. Occasional alarming shouts and yells came from Edmund Norwood in the passenger seat. He feared that one of the gaping craters on the road was about to swallow them up. Meanwhile, Myrid and Irene Thomas, seated in the rear of the van, were calmer. They seemed to be quietly beseeching the Lord for heavenly protection and journeying mercies. å

This was the 1960 rainy season in Northeast Brazil. The four Unevangelised Fields Mission (UFM Worldwide) missionaries had left the town of Piracuruca in Brazil's hinterland early that morning in the hope of reaching the coastal city of Fortaleza by nightfall, a distance of 350 miles. The owner of the van, missionary John Sessoms, was out of the country on furlough and had kindly left his van for Ed's use. Ed and Wesley were certainly putting it to good use by providing transport for Mr & Mrs Thomas, veteran missionaries who were returning home to Wales after serving God for more than three decades in Brazil. This was their last overland trip in Brazil, and they just hoped they would survive it and be able to catch the boat to Liverpool.

Even though the early morning sun had been hot, very soon heavy clouds filled the sky and torrential rain poured down, turning the dust into rivers of mud. Still withal, Wesley motored on, splashing his way through sludge and mire, determined to reach Fortaleza that day.

Besides providing transport for Mr and Mrs Thomas, Wesley and Ed planned to buy needed supplies to take back to Piracuruca. Wesley's wife, Winifred, had given them a shopping list for items that were not readily available back home.

As they neared Fortaleza, the state capital of Ceará on Brazil's Northeastern coast, the road surface improved. and they were able to make steady progress. All four were greatly relieved when the lights of the large city broke on the horizon. Before bedding down that night, they thanked God for answered prayer and travelling mercies. Myrid Thomas was also grateful that he and his wife did not have to make the return journey inland with Wesley and Ed.

After a day of shopping and saying farewell to the veteran missionaries, Wesley and Ed loaded the van and prepared to venture back onto the open road for the return journey to Piracuruca in the inland State of Piauí.

Mindful of the trip over to Fortaleza, the two men set off early in the morning with Wesley behind the wheel again. More tropical downpours increased the already perilous state of the slippery roads. After fifty miles out of Fortaleza the driving conditions worsened. The rain was unrelenting, churning the roads into virtual rivers of mud. It was hard for Wesley to drive at any speed as the van slid, swerved and skidded on the slippery surface. Ed's adrenaline was running high as he helplessly looked on and tried to give occasional advice or make suggestions to Wesley.

Wesley steadily drove on at a moderate speed, but then it happened. Something diverted his attention from the road in front and when he looked around again, the vehicle swerved towards the clay embankment. In a frantic attempt to rectify this, he pulled the steering wheel in the counter direction, but it was too late. The van skidded before careering through a low verge and toppled over on the driver's side and plunged into a lake that was brimming full from the heavy rain. Foul smelling and filthy water gushed into the cabin as the vehicle quickly sank into five feet of water. The two men struggled to get out.

The passenger side of the vehicle was still above the water level and the passenger window was open. Ed was able to open it more so that he could scramble out of the window and onto the vehicle's side. Wesley, now standing above his waist in the filthy water, also struggled to climb up over the seats and steering column to emerge out through the open window.

The two men were soaked, bewildered and dumbfounded. They made their way to the lakeside and back to the muddy road. On the way they lamented about the hazards of their journey, Ed remarked to Wesley, "This is the worst yet." It certainly was. Not only was the van lying in the lake, but also, it was not their vehicle. They wondered how they would ever be able to retrieve it and what had become of the supplies they had loaded on board.

Very soon a jeep approached. When it slowed down, Wesley noticed by the telltale robe that the driver was a priest who was accompanied by two men. Like in the Bible story of the "Good Samaritan", the priest looked over, saw their dilemma, nodded his head and drove on by.

Another vehicle soon came by and several men emerged to offer help in hauling the van out of the lake. They tied a rope to the van and secured the other end to their car. The rope tightened, the wheels of their vehicle spun in the mud, but the submerged van did not budge. These anonymous friends tried again only to have their rope snap in the vain attempt to solve the dilemma.

The men told the missionaries that some men were working at repairing the highway ten miles away. By this time darkness had quickly fallen on them. After an overnight stay in a nearby village, Wesley and Ed set out by bus next morning to solicit help from these workmen.

Typical of Brazilians, the men willingly offered to use their heavy machinery to pull the van from the lake. During the operation, almost twenty-four hours after the accident, Wesley was fearful that they might damage the van. He need not have feared. Ed breathed a sigh of relief when the men skillfully removed the vehicle and set it upright on all four wheels. The filthy water seeped out onto the muddy road. It was a sight to behold.

Amazingly, when they examined the rescued vehicle Wesley discovered that water had not gotten into the petrol tank. However, the old Chevrolet van was a mess. The two missionaries washed the blue vehicle as best they could with the foul-smelling water from the lake. After allowing time for the engine to dry, they were able to get the motor running again.

Wesley confessed to Ed that his nerves were at the breaking point and there was no way he could drive anymore that day. Even though it was late they set off towards home in Piracuruca with Ed in the soggy driving seat. The road was even more perilous in the dark, but Edmund drove slowly along the narrow gauge and treacherous road all through that night. They were too upset for sleep. and their adrenaline kept them alert until daybreak and finally within sight of Piracuruca.

When Ed drove the van up to the mission house both men lifted their hearts to God in praise for His protection through the night. Winnie heard the van arriving. Having expected them to return the previous day, she was anxiously waiting for this moment. When she emerged from the house she was shocked to see the condition of the van and of Wesley and Edmund. She was all the more surprised when Wesley stepped out of the van, got down on his knees and kissed the ground. Undoubtedly she was expecting him to kiss her first.

When Winnie opened her arms to give her husband a welcoming hug she was repelled by the stench. She asked if they had been to a pig yard, for they stank of pig slurry. Winnie asked, "What did you kiss the ground for?"

"I was never so glad to get back home again to Piracuruca," said Wesley. "There was a time when I thought I would not see it or you again."

Winnie asked about the supplies they bought in Fortaleza. Both men looked at each other. Wesley held up what had been left of the sack of sugar. The contents had melted away in the water and the other supplies were totally ruined.

After a wash, a change of clothing and a good warm meal of rice and beans, Wesley and Edmund sat down and recounted to Winnie all that had happened since they had left her several days earlier. It truly was "the worst ever."

Recounting their eventful journey to Winnie helped them recognize how God had protected them from what might have been a fatal accident. It would have been even more horrific if it had happened when Mr and Mrs Thomas had been with them. Before retiring that night they lifted their hearts to God in praise and prayer. They also recognized that someone must have been praying for them.

That night Wesley Gould could not help recollecting how often God had preserved him. He was convinced that God still had work for him to do. That work had begun many years earlier.

CHAPTER 2

Back to the Future

LIFE BEGAN FOR Wesley Gould in Mourneview Street, Portadown, Northern Ireland. He had two siblings, James his older brother, and Margaret his younger sister. In those post-World War I years, life was not easy, and money was scarce. Their hard-working father turned his hand to many things to bring in a livable income for his wife and children. He worked as a hackler and became a foreman in the linen making process. He also worked for some years for the Co-Op as a horse-and-cart bread-server in the town. On top of all of this, he was also a part-time farmer.

Besides caring for her three children at home, Mrs Gould was a busy dressmaker, making garments for her family and others. The children attended Thomas Street Public Elementary School behind the Methodist Church. Wesley was by no means an angelic pupil. He still smarts from the memory of several canings he suffered when corporal punishment was permissible at school.

Mrs Gould showered love on all her family, poured her heart out in constant prayer for them and tried to control James' erratic behaviour. Although James broke his mother's heart at times, this sad situation bonded Wesley and Margaret closer together in an enduring brother-and-sister relationship.

This Christian family belonged to and faithfully attended Thomas Street Methodist Church. Throughout his childhood, Wesley attended the morning and afternoon Sunday Schools as well as the two church services every Sunday. Those early Bible lessons made a deep impression on Wesley for the rest of his life.

Another Sunday School experience also left a marked imprint on Wesley. As soon as morning Sunday School finished the boys dashed for the door to see who could be out of the building first. On one Sunday morning, an eager ten-year-old Wesley was first out through the door. Instead of rushing down the staircase. he knew that the quickest way to descend was to slide down the banister. He was so eager to be first that morning that when he jumped onto the banister he over-balanced and fell to the stone steps below. Young Wesley was knocked unconscious and remembered nothing about it until he opened his eyes in the doctor's surgery sometime later. Apart from a nasty cut inside his mouth, Wesley escaped serious injury. He still recalls that he might have been killed that day, but he believes the Lord preserved his life for a purpose.

Wesley left school after his fourteenth birthday, as did most children at that time. Employment was not plentiful, but Wesley's father secured a job for his son in Greaves' Weaving Factory in Portadown. Right from the outset, he hated his job. He could not stand the heat in the building or the constant noise of the looms. He detested it all, but money was scarce, and there seemed to be no alternative for him.

This revulsion to work resulted in Wesley forsaking Sunday School, church attendance and anything related to religion. He and his friends Alfie Watson and Billy Gibson became engrossed in outdoor activities: playing football, swimming in the River Bann and attending the local cinema on Saturday evenings.

Although he did not attend church he knew that his mother never gave up praying for her children. After Wesley celebrated his nineteenth birthday he recalled hearing a preacher say, "If you are not converted before you are twenty years old, your heart will become so hardened that the chances of becoming a Christian will be greatly diminished." This sobering statement played on Wesley's mind. He had never lost the awareness that he was a sinner or the fear that if he died without Christ, he would be lost in hell forever.

With his twentieth birthday quickly approaching Wesley decided to attend an evangelistic mission being conducted in Portadown by two Brethren evangelists, Duff and Allen. All that he had learned at church and Sunday School about sin, eternity and salvation came flooding back to his mind. At the end of the meeting on 20th August 1940, Wesley asked the Lord Jesus Christ to save him.

He was the only convert of that mission, but although it happened at the Brethren mission, Wesley was not admitted into fellowship at the local Brethren Assembly; therefore, he returned to the Gould's family's church. The Rev. R. H. Gallagher was delighted to welcome the young convert and soon conscripted him into a host of church activities. Before long Wesley was teaching a Sunday School class and became an active member of the Boy's Brigade at Thomas Street Methodist Church. He was introduced to a Local Preachers' Study Course with other friends from the church, and in due time they all graduated. The Rev. Gallagher soon had these budding preachers conducting services in the circuit of the seven Methodist Churches for which he was responsible.

Becoming a Christian not only gave Wesley a new impetus for living a new life in Christ, he also changed jobs. He was glad to leave the weaving factory and become an apprentice cabinetmaker.

His preaching commitments and church activities constrained Wesley to read more, not only his Bible but also missionary biographies. He had always been fascinated by the life of David Livingstone. He was greatly challenged when he read the story of Hudson Taylor founding the China Inland Mission and the story of John G Paton's work in the South Sea Islands. Since his childhood, he had had a desire to be a missionary and that desire was deepened when the church congregation sang:

> Can we whose souls are lighted,
> With wisdom from on high,
> Can we to men benighted,
> The lamp of life deny?

Wesley was convinced that the reason why God had spared his life on that day when he fell over the banister to the stone floor below after Sunday School was that he should serve God one day as a missionary.

Those early impressions helped Wesley formulate a decision one night at a church concert. There was no missionary speaker, but on that night Wesley felt that God was speaking to his heart and asking him to do something – to give his life to become a missionary.

At twenty-two years of age, Wesley said "Yes" to God and surrendered his life to Christ for Christian service wherever that might be.

CHAPTER 3

Stepping Out

THE METHODIST CHURCH'S Local Preachers' Course provided Wesley with some experience in Christian work as opportunities arose. With a longing in his heart to preach the Gospel in the "regions beyond" where thousands had never heard the message, he felt his need for more Bible training. After some enquiries, Wesley learned that a new Bible school had been opened in Belfast the previous year.

Mr and Mrs Robert McKnight had opened the Belfast Bible School and Missionary Training Home in 1943. Mr McKnight, a former headmaster, and his wife Rosalind had a heart for missions but were unable to go overseas. They felt called and constrained to help others do what they could not do; therefore, they opened the Bible School in Belfast's Windsor Avenue.

World War II was drawing to a close, and many young soldiers were returning from the battlefront. Wesley knew that the Lord was recruiting him for another conflict, a spiritual one. With that conviction in his heart, he applied to and was accepted by Belfast Bible School to begin studies in September 1944.

Although at first, he was a little apprehensive, Wesley soon found that he had much in common with other young people at the college who had felt a similar call on their lives and a need to study the Bible. Among his newly found college colleagues were Robert Mackey who went to Liberia and became the international leader of the Worldwide Evangelization Crusade (WEC), Billy McIlfatrick who went to India with OMS, Minnie Bell (Minnie Khasho) who went to Syria with the

Reformed Presbyterian Church, Donald Wilson who served God with WEC and David Ross who later became a UFM colleague with Wesley in Brazil.

Wesley soon settled down to study the Scriptures and related Bible subjects. The Rev S. T. Nelson from Magherafelt Methodist Church was one of his favourite lecturers. However, he also found that Mr and Mrs McKnight were very strict disciplinarians. The students were encouraged to be totally focused on their studies of the Scriptures and on their calling to the work. Romance and relationships between students were not permitted and even relationships outside of college were frowned upon.

These restrictions posed no problem for Wesley until he visited Lisburn Road Methodist Church one Sunday morning. Billy McIlfatrick, Don Wilson, and Wesley were all Methodists. For that reason, they went to the morning worship service at the nearby Lisburn Road Methodist Church. After the service, the congregation milled out onto the footpath outside the church. Just then, Billy McIlfatrick spied someone he knew. It was Winifred Dundas who came from near Billy's home in County Fermanagh. Winifred, also a Methodist, had worked for the Ministry of Agriculture at Stormont but was assigned to government offices at Balmoral Avenue. She told Billy that she had been staying in lodgings near the church for the last two years.

Billy, glad to see someone from Fermanagh, introduced Winifred to his colleagues, Donald and Wesley. That was the first time Wesley and Winifred had ever met, and they could never have imagined the great future God had planned for them or the outcome of that first encounter. This was not by chance, this was a match, planned and made in heaven. Billy encouraged Winnie to attend the evening Bible Study Classes at the Belfast Bible College. In the back of her mind Winnie already had the intention of serving God as a missionary, and although training to be a nurse was already in her plans, she decided to accept this invitation to study the Bible at the college several evenings each week.

Back at the college, some banter ensued among the students about "the girl" Wesley had met at church. At the weekends the young couple met up for outings, although it was not romance at this stage. When news of this got to Mr and Mrs McKnight's ears she lectured Wesley very severely about being distracted from his calling and to put this nonsense out of his head. Wesley tried, but Winifred had already stolen a piece of his heart. Although he tried to keep it under wraps, it was not easy.

Mr McKnight was more softly spoken and more diplomatic in his approach. He called Wesley aside to have a private word with him. Lifting his index finger up to his eye, he said to Wesley, "I want to tell you a true story. In the village where I was a student teacher, there was a lad known as the village idiot. On a particular day, a pack of hounds was on a hunt for a fox. The boy did not want the hounds to catch the fox so he tied a red herring, a kipper, to a string and dragged it along a lane until he came to a gate. He rubbed the red herring across the gate and into a field hoping that the scent would distract the hounds. He might have been known as an idiot, but he knew exactly what he was doing."

Mrs McKnight had more to add. "You are going to Brazil. Look at Horace Banner, he is going to be here next week. He has sacrificed marriage that he might be able to devote his time to the Kayapo Indians."

When Horace Banner got up to speak to the students the following week, the first thing he said was, "I have just become engaged, and Eva and I hope to be married soon. She is looking forward to working in Brazil, and I am really pleased to have a wife." There were some hidden smiles.

While studying in Belfast Wesley repeatedly sought God with an open heart for guidance. He was willing to go where God might lead, but where would that be? At college, the students were exposed to missionary speakers and encouraged to read missionary biographies. Reading about Horace and Eva Banner's work amongst Brazil's indigenous Indians and the report of the martyrdom of the Three Freds in their attempt to reach the Kayapo Indians, challenged Wesley deeply.

That challenge constrained Wesley to make further preparation for God's work abroad by enrolling at the Missionary School of Medicine in London. During that year Wesley learned about the rudiments of medicine, tropical diseases, minor surgeries and dental extractions. These provided Wesley with knowledge and skills that he would put to good use in future days.

Throughout this time, Wesley kept in touch with Winifred Dundas who had resigned from the civil service to take up nursing training in Dublin. Meanwhile, he had been praying about which doors might open to him. His long conversations with his fellow student, David Ross, helped him be persuaded to apply to the UFM for their work in Brazil late in 1947.

After submitting application papers and references and undergoing interviews, Wesley was accepted as a UFM missionary candidate for Brazil. He spent a little while at the UFM headquarters in East London before returning home to engage in deputation work and raise support for his missionary future.

Just at that time, a new young minister had arrived at Edenderry Presbyterian Church, Rev William Craig. Wesley attended a cottage meeting near his home that was organised by his neighbour, Mr Burnett. Wesley met the Rev Craig at that meeting and for the next thirty-nine years, the Rev Craig became a prayer partner and great supporter of Wesley's missionary enterprises. Wesley was grateful and encouraged by the financial and prayer support he received from Christians of all denominations.

At Wesley's valedictory service in Portadown in December 1948, Wesley spoke on the Bible text: "Other sheep I have which are not of this fold, them also I must bring" (John 11:16). At the end of the meeting a young man, Bertie Wright, a well-known football player, trusted Christ as Saviour and went on to serve God in the Christian Endeavour movement.

At Bible college Wesley had often heard it remarked, "There is many a slip between the cup and the lip, and there is many a slip between the call and the ship." Wesley experienced the irony of that saying when he arrived in Liverpool to embark on the Booth Line cargo ship, the *Dunstan*, which was to sail on Christmas Day. When Wesley checked into the Booth Line office at Liverpool docks he was really shocked and frustrated to be told that the ship was not leaving from Liverpool. It was due to leave from London, and he would have to embark there.

Wesley was thrown with this news. Thankfully, he did not have a lot of baggage. He had one small hand-held trunk that Joe Wright had given him. Joe told him that it belonged to Fred Wright who had been killed by the Kayapo Indians in Brazil. While he was musing on how he was going to travel to London his friend and soon would be his colleague in Brazil, overheard what was happening and saw Wesley's predicament. His fiancé, Dorothy Reese, was returning home to London after visiting her future in-laws in Belfast. David and Dorothy invited Wesley to travel with her on the train to London where he could stay with her parents.

After his unplanned trip to London and a very welcome overnight with the Reese family, Wesley, with his trunk in hand, made his way to the Booth Line office at the London docks. On his arrival, a clerk told him, "The *Dunstan* sailed last night to Liverpool. From there it will depart for Brazil."

If Wesley had been bewildered before in Liverpool, he was really frustrated now, for he felt he was being led on a merry dance. He had to rush across London to Euston Station where he caught another train back to Liverpool. He was glad when he finally boarded the ship and was securely in his cabin.

On the last day of 1948, Wesley set sail from Liverpool for Brazil. This was the maiden voyage of the new Booth Line cargo ship, the *Dunstan*. He was conscious that the ordination of the Saviour's nail-pierced hand was upon him.

CHAPTER 4

Welcome to Brazil

THE *DUNSTAN* TOOK almost a month to conduct Wesley and the other four passengers to Brazil. En route they visited such exotic ports as Lisbon, Madeira, Tenerife and Barbados before arriving off the coast of Brazil. Even before they could see Brazil over the horizon, Wesley noticed that the frenzied waves of the Atlantic breaking the bow of the boat had been transformed from its usual aquamarine water to a muddy brown colour. This was because the mighty River Amazon forces its fresh water and silt-filled flow more than seventy miles out into the Atlantic.

Soon Wesley saw the palm-tree lined and sandy coast of Brazil emerge over the horizon. Under the guidance of the ship's pilot, the vessel slowly entered the River Amazon and then up the river to dock at the capital city of Pará, Belém, ninety miles inland. As Wesley prepared to disembark the thought struck him, "This is the land to which God has called me."

Little could have prepared Wesley for the culture shock that he encountered over the next few weeks: the oppressive heat, the draining humidity, the tropical downpours, the sounds, the smells, the change of diet, and to crown it all, the Portuguese that he found difficult to learn.

Charles Sargenson, the UFM field leader in Brazil, was there to welcome Wesley and take him to the mission headquarters. After introducing himself to the new missionary Charles gave Wesley the customary Brazilian abraço, a tight embrace. He asked Wesley where his baggage was. Wesley pointed to one small cabin trunk. The field leader could not hide his surprise, for he was used to missionaries arriving with more than a ton of baggage.

At the mission base, a large bungalow on the 14 de Março Street, Wesley was introduced to four other new missionaries who had just arrived on the field. All of them, like Wesley, were single men in their twenties, three from Canada and one from the USA.

For the next nine months Orvel Yontz, Ted Laskowski, Bob Hawkings, Will Jack and Wesley tried to come to terms with masculine and feminine nouns, conjugations of regular and irregular verbs with their tenses and moods, memorizing them and trying to get their tongues around the new phonetics. What annoyed Wesley most was that Ted Laskowski was able to sail through the written and oral exams while he struggled and was left scratching his head.

Like everyone learning a new language Wesley learned to laugh at his mistakes. It was part of language learning. He found that most Brazilians were too kind to laugh at the missionary's mistakes in his presence, but they often doubled up with laughter afterwards.

Little by little the candidates gained some measure of proficiency with Portuguese. They visited various churches, the leprosy colony, and several riverside preaching points, always being encouraged to speak only in Portuguese.

Even though Wesley did not feel that he attained the fluency of Portuguese that he needed to preach after five months in Belém, Charles Sargenson, the field leader, asked him to join Alf and Margaret Sutton in Santa Inêz.

Wesley had never met Mr and Mrs Sutton but learned that they were an English couple that had been serving God in Santa Inêz for about ten years. He also discovered that Santa Inêz was a village in the interior of Maranhão in Brazil's northeastern region.

Very soon Wesley packed his belongings and was on his way by ship from Belém around Brazil's northeast coast to São Luiz, Maranhão's State capital. The sailing took less than two days. Mr and Mrs Sutton and their two children, Geoffrey and Sylvia, were already in São Luiz to buy supplies and wait for the arrival of their new colleague. After all their initial welcomes and introductions, Wesley joined the Suttons to board a smaller river steamer that transported them for three days up the River Pindaré Mirim to eventually dock at Central, the nearest river port to Santa Inêz.

During the journey, Wesley became more acquainted with the Suttons and their two young children. As the steamer made steady progress up the river, at times it seemed like they were slipping through a corridor of impenetrable forest on each side which was occasionally broken by small riverside dwellings and open fields of grazing cattle. At night Wesley was fascinated to sleep in a hammock and soon found it to be very comfortable.

On arrival at Central, they unloaded their baggage and supplies. There was no motorized transport to take them and their belongings to Santa Inez. There was not even a passable road that would allow vehicles to travel the five miles to the town. They loaded the baggage onto mules for the trip. Wesley was a bit hesitant about riding a mule so he walked alongside the animals. He would have to learn to ride a mule quickly, for this would be his means of transport for some time to come.

After nearly two hours trekking Wesley saw the town's wide street lined with small mud-stucco houses covered with palm-leaf roofs. Soon they unpacked their baggage at the old mission house next door to the church that Alf Sutton had built. It did not take Wesley long to unpack, for he had arrived in Brazil with little luggage. After he hung his clothes in his room, he was ready to explore the town.

Wesley discovered that Santa Inêz was little more than a village with approximately 500 of a population; the majority of the residents were of African descent. During the early part of the nineteenth century, the Portuguese imported many slaves from their African colonies to this part of Brazil to work on the sugar plantations.

During Alf and Margaret Sutton's years in the town, they not only led quite a few people to faith in Christ, but he had also built a small church. Alf was a bricklayer, a skill unheard of in that region at that time. When he decided to construct the church building he wanted to do so with bricks. There were no brick buildings in the town and no one had ever heard of bricks. Most houses in Santa Inêz were built with mud. Interwoven sticks formed the frame of the house and then clay was mixed with straw and compressed onto the frame. The muddy structure dried out in the hot sun.

Alf was not only a pioneer missionary, he also led the way for bricklaying in that part of Maranhão. He taught some local men how to make bricks from clay, fire them in a kiln and have them ready for the church. Alf did the bricklaying. The construction was such a local novelty that when it was nearing completion, people came from far and near to see the building collapse. No one believed that anything built on blocks of clay could withstand the tropical rain and heat. Of course, Alf proved them all wrong, and very soon bricklaying was introduced to the region.

A feature that Alf included in the first evangelical church building in Santa Inez was a baptismal tank. Locals had never seen believers being immersed in water. The immersion was then followed by hymn singing and great rejoicing. Alf, a Baptist, also baptized Wesley at the Santa Inez church.

A few days after Wesley arrived some of the believers were going to Bom Futuro, a village about fifteen miles away to conduct some Gospel meetings. Wesley volunteered to go with them. The only means of transport was on mule back. A few of the believers said the new missionary would never make it on a mule. However, Wesley finally persuaded them to let him go. He rode "Old beauty", as she was incorrectly called, all the way without any serious mishaps.

Senhor Pedro, a Christian man who lived in Bom Futuro, welcomed the group with the customary *abraço*, a tight embrace. While his daughters pounded the rice in a mortar for the evening meal, Wesley decided to visit some of the neighbouring houses to invite people to the meeting in Pedro's house that evening.

Just as Wesley arrived at one door the man of the house was about to go to his plantation to sow rice. Wesley engaged him in conversation about the Gospel. Their exchange went on for a quite while with the result that the man had been detained too long, and therefore, had to defer from planting rice until the following day. The man was very upset that he had been delayed so much, and he blamed Wesley for it.

Years later, Wesley learned that there was a sequel to this incident. Senhor José Madeiro, who later became a pastor, was a good friend to Wesley in Santa Inêz and often helped preach in the church and lead Sunday School. He was part of that group that took Wesley on his first visit to Bom Futuro. While back visiting in the town years later, he met a man who asked him if he did not recognize this stranger. José admitted that he could not recollect ever meeting the man before.

At this, the man said, "Do you remember back in 1949 when you and a wee missionary came to visit Bom Futuro, and you came to my house and talked to me for a long time about salvation? Well, I was so furious with you that day. You upset my plans to sow rice, and I felt I had lost vital time, a whole day. I was so angry that I made up my mind to harm both of you that night. With my bush knife well sharpened, I circled round and round Senhor Pedro's house during the meeting, hoping for an opportunity to attack you both, but it did not work out. I want to tell you that I am a Christian now, and all my family also accepted Christ as Saviour."

Wesley had no doubt that someone, in some place and at that very moment must have been praying for them. The Lord not only restrained the murderer's hand, God's glorious grace brought the man to repentance and faith in Jesus Christ.

Each week Alf Sutton helped Wesley prepare messages in Portuguese while his wife, Margaret, home-schooled their two children. Just as Wesley was taking his first faltering steps of preaching in Portuguese, Mrs Sutton became ill. There was no medical help for her in town so the Sutton family had to leave Santa Inêz and travel to the mission base in Belém for treatment.

Their departure left Wesley alone in the old rambling mission house.

CHAPTER 5

Boys from County Armagh

B EING LEFT ALONE in the interior town of Santa Inêz had its advantages and disadvantages. There were times when Wesley felt lonely – especially with no one to whom he could speak English. At the same time, this became a blessing, for he was forced to speak and preach in Portuguese all the time, and this greatly helped his fluency.

Senhor Lino Santos, his wife, Isabel, and their three daughters lived next door to the mission house. They were all Christians. Dona Isobel cooked Wesley's meals, and Senhor Lino became a very close companion who helped in the church and often went with him to various preaching points. The three young girls had plenty of fun and noise by singing choruses and playing nearby. After a short while, Wesley agreed that Senhor Lino and his family should move into the mission house.

Traditional Brazilian holidays and Roman Catholic Saint days always attracted people from the interior and brought some excitement to the town. One event that stands out in Wesley's memory while living alone in Santa Inêz is "Dia De Mansar Os Cavalos," or "Taming the Horses Day."

The day began by professional *vaqueros*, cowboys, riding untamed horses through the village. To "break" the horse, they would ride the steed at speed up and down the main street for about two hundred metres in each direction. The cowboys lashed and whipped the poor horses and dug their spurs into their bodies until they bled. The on-looking crowd roared and cheered as each horse galloped past. The galloping seemed to go on endlessly until some of the blood-soaked horses collapsed on the street.

Wesley had never seen anything like it and was fascinated to see all the excitement amongst the crowds of people. Foolishly the young Irish missionary asked one of the trainers if he could mount and ride his horse. The trainer placed a whip in Wesley's hand, helped him up onto the horse and fixed his feet in the stirrups. With that Wesley gave then horse a gentle tap. The horse immediately dashed down the road at a very high speed knocking Wesley back in the saddle. Nevertheless, he was able to hang on until the horse stopped abruptly at the end of the street. The horse's sudden halt threw Wesley out of the saddle but his left foot was still caught in the stirrup. The horse then ran around in circles dragging and kicking at Wesley while it did so. Wesley's predicament soon caught the attention of the people who gathered round to see the horse making a fool of the foreigner.

When the horse finally stopped, Wesley was able to free himself from the stirrup. After he dusted himself down, he walked home, thankful to the Lord for his protection. He thought that if the people at home could see him now; however, there was no one in Santa Inêz with whom he could share his story in English.

At the next church meeting, he used the incident to contrast his experience with that of the Lord Jesus Christ who rode an ass into Jerusalem. He emphasized that no one had ever ridden or tamed that colt. However, when Jesus sat on the animal, He changed its nature so that the ass meekly bore Christ through the multitudes that were waving their palms and crying Hosannas to the Saviour. Wesley told the congregation that through grace, Jesus Christ was still changing the nature of people. He can make them new creatures through the new birth.

After almost five months on his own Wesley was joined in Santa Inêz by a new missionary fresh out of language school, Charlie Thompson. Neither man knew the other before they met each other in Santa Inez even though Charlie's home in the small village of

Annaghmore was less than seven miles away from where Wesley had been reared in County Armagh.

Charlie, like Wesley, had been to the Missionary School of Medicine in London, and in the absence of any doctor or dentist in town, they put their limited knowledge and experience to use in treating the sick and extracting teeth. They also provided these services wherever they travelled. Both men taught Lino some dental skills. When Wesley eventually left town he gave his dental instruments to Lino who was able to use them to help earn a living.

They also introduced some novel events for the church's children and young people. They organised a picnic on the grassy banks of the River Pindaré where they had a wonderful day with games, races, and plenty to eat. It was a memorable time for the church families and the two Irishmen.

Together Wesley and Charlie pastored the church in Santa Inêz. Although money was not plentiful, both men bought a horse each so they could travel to various distant preaching points.

On one occasion they travelled on horseback to conduct a meeting in a small village, Três Poços. After a good meeting, they planned to return to Santa Inêz the next day. Some folk told them that there was a shortcut by crossing the Lago Verde (Green Lake). They decided to take this advice and go home that way. The Lago Verde was about a hundred yards wide but they were told that there was a shallow part of the lake where the horses would be able to cross. Although the local people knew exactly where this shallow area was, the men were not so sure.

Charlie's horse was older as well as being quiet and steady, but Wesley's steed was very easily frightened, especially when it got into water and mud. Charlie was able to ride his horse through to the other side with no trouble. Not so with Wesley. As soon as he rode the horse into the lake it began to buck and struggle. Before they knew it, they were off the beaten track and into deeper water and mud. Soon the horse threw Wesley off its back dumping him into the dirty water. Into the bargain, the saddle straps broke allowing the saddlebag with clothes, Bible, hymnbook and everything else, to fall into the water.

Wesley struggled to his feet and managed to retrieve the saddle from the lake. He placed the sodden saddle back on the horse and secured it as best he could. He then mounted the steed once more, but after a few yards, the horse threw Wesley and the saddle with its contents also. There was no way he was going to try to ride the horse through the water, so he grabbed the halter and dragged the frightened horse behind him to the other side of the lake.

Once he got his horse to solid ground he secured it to a tree before throwing off his muddy and wet clothes. Wesley then started back into the lake to retrieve the saddle. On his way, he bumped into a bush and upset a hornet's nest. Immediately a swarm of angry hornets flew out to attack Wesley and defend their territory. Poor Wesley, already feeling a little sorry for himself after being soaked and dumped in the mud, was now stung on his head, his arms and shoulders. Notwithstanding all this, he finally got the saddle out of the lake, placed it on his head and returned to his shivering horse.

While all this had been going on Charlie had been sitting at the side of the lake enjoying the whole episode at Wesley's expense. Charlie teased Wesley when he said that while waiting for his beleaguered friend he had been reading his Bible in Psalm 23. He said he was amused at how fitting this Psalm had been for this incident at the Green Lake. "He makes me to lie down in green pastures, He leads me beside still waters!"

The two men arrived home that night, tired, hungry and dirty, but very happy in that they had been able to preach the Word of God to the people in Três Poços.

CHAPTER 6

Reaching Out

THE TWO YOUNG County Armagh missionaries, Wesley Gould and Charlie Thompson, were keen to reach out further and further with the good news of the Gospel. For some time they had contemplated a visit to the Guajajara Indians in the Sapucaia on the upper River Pindaré Mirim.

As far back as the 1930s, there had been a mission station there. Mr and Mrs Fred Roberts from Australia, who had arrived in Brazil in 1925, worked amongst these indigenous people. Sadly, Mrs Roberts was stricken down with fever and died while working with the tribe. She was buried there. Her husband joined missionaries, Fred Dawson, also an Australian, and Fred Wright from Northern Ireland, to reach the Kayapo Indians on the River Xingu with the Gospel. The Kayapo Indians killed all three missionaries in 1936.

Fenton Hall, who also came from Northern Ireland and before becoming a missionary, had been a champion boxer in the British Army, also died amongst these Guajajara Indians in the Sapucaia less than six months after arriving in Brazil.

To reach the Indians in the Sapucaia, Wesley and Charlie hired a canoe with two men to help them. They also hired a young lad to be their cook. On the 27th January 1951, the party left Santa Inêz for their trip. They expected the trip would take about six days. Paddling the canoe against a strong upstream current was hard work. At times they had to cut their way through fallen trees that had become a barrier across the river. They noticed that there were no riverside dwellings until they reached the Indian village.

With no forest homes available, the men slung their hammocks between the trees at night. It was important to keep a fire burning all night to ward off jaguars and other wild animals in case they came for a midnight feast of human meat. Wesley sensed a strange feeling of isolation and loneliness in the virgin jungle. This was especially the case during the long hours of darkness when many unsettling sounds of insects, birds, and animals echo in the stillness of the night. The cries of the howler monkey put a shiver up their spine, for it sounded like a child wailing in agony.

Insects also are legion in these remote and sparsely inhabited areas. By day innumerable swarms of sand flies tortured the intrepid travellers as they sat in the canoe in the hot sun hour after hour. Each bite left a little bump on the victim's skin, and this soon began to itch. After Wesley got hundreds of these tiny bites, he thought he would go crazy. At sunset, it seemed that the sand flies went off duty only for the dreaded mosquitoes to take over for the night shift. The two men knew that some of these mosquitoes were carriers of malaria, one of the most dreaded and fatal tropical diseases.

Wesley and Charlie's troubles were compounded when they discovered that their hired crew had deceived them. They had promised them a good canoe, but instead, the one that was brought was too small for five people. Into the bargain, the canoe leaked, and this meant that someone had to be constantly bailing water out of the canoe to prevent it from sinking. Furthermore, the hired men had also promised to provide a good supply of food for the journey, but after the second day, the rice and beans ran out. All they had for the rest of the journey was some farinha (granules of roasted mandioca). They even ran out of coffee.

To survive the trip after their supplies ran out, one of the Brazilians caught some fish in the river. They used a stick as a skewer to cook the catch over an open fire. Farther upriver the Brazilians went hunting and caught an *anta*, a tapir. The two missionaries found the roasted tapir meat to be as tough as shoe leather. They much preferred the fresh fish from the river. Later, when the Brazilian men caught and roasted a monkey, Wesley and Charlie ate it, for they knew that beggars could not be choosers. There was nothing else on the menu.

Paddling upriver all day in the hot sun was exhausting and left the men physically drained at the end of the day. At midday and before dark they stopped to cool off and wash in the river. In one place the young cook stripped off all his clothing and dove into the muddy river, ignoring any likelihood of encountering an unsuspecting crocodile or being bitten by a piranha fish. Wesley was amused that when the young man emerged from his naked swim the first item of clothing he put on was his cap.

One day as they passed the forest's edge they saw a large Surucucu snake, similar to the Anaconda, twined around a tree stump. The snake's swollen tummy indicated that it was digesting a large meal. One of the Brazilians shot the snake and then trailed it from the tree onto the ground. The Brazilians did not take time to open the snake to see what it had swallowed. However, when they were coming back down river, a week or later, they only found the bones of the snake. The vultures had devoured the carcass, leaving only its extended skeleton. In the midst of the snake's bones, they saw the remains of a giant turtle, a tartaruga. Obviously, through time the strong juices in the snake's stomach would have softened the hard turtle-shell if the snake had not been killed.

After several days of laborious paddling up river, the party finally arrived at the Sapucaia Indian village. They were disappointed to find that only a handful of Indians were living in two separate villages. Most of those that Wesley and Charlie met were sick. The old Sapucaia chief was very ill with malaria. The missionaries were able to give him some medicine in the hope that it would stop the malarial cycles of fever and rigors. At one time there had been hundreds of these Indians in the Sapucaia. Sadly, over the years an epidemic of various sicknesses without the proper medicines had resulted in most of the tribe having died.

After treating the sick, the two missionaries were able to give a simple Gospel message to those who understood Portuguese. Most of these Indians had never heard of Jesus and probably would never hear again. Wesley and Charlie's hearts went out to these dear souls who were living in spiritual darkness. They were reluctant to leave them, for there was no one to give them a better understanding of the message of forgiveness and salvation through Christ.

Wesley and Charlie searched in the forest to try to find the graves of Mrs Roberts and Fenton Hall. Their search was in vain. The Indians had no idea where the missionaries had been buried. However, the two men did find the remains of the house where Mr and Mrs Roberts had lived.

Fred Roberts wrote home to his friends in New South Wales, Australia, of the rigors and dangers of their early days trying to reach lost souls in these forests:

> Many times I have had to make a journey with a high fever and a splitting headache. Then one often comes to a swamp that takes half an hour to cross. We are glad when we get to the other side, to be able to crawl out of the foul-smelling water, infested often with the cannibal fish, electric eels, stinging ray, and the dreaded Anaconda snake, so huge that it can swallow a man with ease.

> But, for the missionary travelling alone, except for the company of an Indian guide, there is a harder experience still. As the night closes about him there is an awful sense of loneliness and dread. We have known missionaries in such conditions to throw themselves on the ground, and sob after sob would break forth from an overwrought heart.

Wesley and Charlie bowed their heads and remembered the great price that had been paid by a missionary martyr, his wife, and colleague, who had passed that way and made the greatest sacrifice of devotion to reach the lost for Christ.

CHAPTER 7

On the Move

WESLEY AND CHARLIE had worked well together in Santa Inêz. They travelled widely throughout the region preaching the Gospel wherever they got an opening. They did encounter opposition from local clergy, but this did not deter them. They also trained young Brazilians for the work and were encouraged to see some of them develop into pastors and evangelists.

Both men put their practical skills to use in completing the church building in Santa Inêz. They also spent time renovating a small church in the neighbouring town of Pindaré Mirim. Other missionaries had founded the work there in former years, but they had moved away, and the church building had been closed for two years. Wesley and Charlie repaired and restored it, and afterwards, believers from Santa Inêz travelled over to clean it. In August 1950 the building was reopened for the preaching of the Gospel. Each week several believers travelled to Pindaré Mirim to conduct the services there and maintain the witness in the town.

Wesley's two-year tenure in Santa Inêz came to an end when pastor David Lopes was sent to pastor the church. The UFM Field Council asked Charlie to work alongside the new pastor but, Wesley was transferred from the town to Altamira on the River Xingu in the State of Pará. The Xingu is one of the five tributaries that are over 1,000 miles long.

Wesley was sorry to leave his friends at the church as well as his neighbours in the town and his close colleague Charlie Thompson. His two years in Maranhão had been a good learning curve for him, but now he looked to new challenges in Pará.

Jesuit missionaries originally settled in Altamira when they cleared the forest to build a Catholic mission centre on the banks of the Panelas Igarapé. African slaves were brought to cut through the forest and open the way to the River Xingu. In 1880 immigration from various parts of the world enlarged the settlement until it was declared to be the Municipality of Altamira on 6th November 1911.

The Kayapo Indian tribe was the largest indigenous group on the long stretch of the River Xingu. Although they were one tribe they lived in scattered villages throughout the region. The Kayapo covered their entire bodies in a black paint derived from local plants. They believed that their ancestors learned from insects so for that reason they painted their bodies to mimic the creepy crawlies so they could better communicate with the Spirit that exists everywhere. Their black bodies also allow them to blend into their surroundings when hunting in the forests. The Kayapo men use large disks inserted into their lower lips and adorn their hair with feathers.

In the 1930s UFM missionaries, Fred Dawson, Fred Wright and Fred Roberts, spent more than a year trying to make friendly contact with this tribe in order to introduce the Gospel to them. In May 1935 from Altamira, they travelled four days by launch and then fifteen more by canoe up the River Nova Olinda. They had to negotiate the dangerous rapids on the way to the Kayapos. They did not return.

Fred Wright wrote home to his family in Northern Ireland:

> At the moment of writing, we are at the last outpost of civilisation. Within two days we shall be up to the Riozlnho. We have been two weeks travelling up the Xingu River, and we are lumps from head to foot from the bites of terrible insects.

Another heroic message from Fred Wright said:

> Within a few weeks we shall be outside the pale of
> civilisation; then we shall purchase a canoe, fit the motor,
> don coats of galvanised iron, and the search for Indians
> will begin. We shall be the first white men to intrude upon
> the freedom of the Indians. Therefore, we are fully aware
> that, humanly speaking, we are already as good as dead
> men.

When the three missionaries did not return, the mission asked Horace
Banner and Willie (Jock) Johnston to travel to the Xingu in search for
them in April 1936. When they reached the River Nova Olinda Horace
and Jock found the men's kit and the metal sheets with which the three
men must have hoped to protect themselves. Beyond the rapids, the
two searchers came upon the place where the three had slept and had
cut their initials on a tree trunk. Five days later they reached the Smoke
Falls where they saw their battered canoe. A heap of what had been
clothing was found nearby.

In the wake of the martyrdom of these three missionaries, Horace
Banner dedicated his life to taking the Gospel to the Kayapos. On their
return journey to safety, Horace recorded that he turned to the second
chapter of Ezekiel and read; "And thou, son of man, be not afraid of
them … be not afraid of their words, nor dismayed at their looks …
Thou shalt speak my words unto them."

These words led Horace and Eva to set up their base in Altamira
and dedicate their lives to not only make friendly contact with these
Indians but also to evangelise and eventually establish the first Kayapo
church.

Wesley joined Cecil and Grace McMullen who also came from
Northern Ireland, at the mission house in Altamira. On arrival, he felt
he was walking on history, for it was from here that colleagues and a
fellow Irish man had passed through on their way to martyrdom.

Cecil and Wesley travelled together on the River Xingu in a large canoe with an outboard motor. Their aim was to reach many families who lived along the rivers with the Gospel message. These expeditions with Cecil were cut short after a few months when Mrs McMullen became ill. As a consequence, Cecil and Grace had to move to Belém for medical treatment. Their departure left Wesley on his own again.

Even though he was alone, Wesley continued to journey on the River Xingu to preach the Gospel to the riverside dwellers. He decided to go a day's journey down the river to what was commonly known as the Gold Mines. Several men were still searching for gold on a small river where some precious metals were reputed to have been found. These men spent their days panning the sand from the riverbed in the hope of sudden riches.

Wesley invited Chico, a believer who lived in Altamira, to travel with him and help in the meetings. Travel down the river was quite easy because they benefitted from the swift current. At the same time, it was dangerous when they had to pass through the rapids where rocks and submerged tree stumps were a constant hazard. After they survived the rapids, somehow, water got into the outboard motor. The engine kept going, but it spluttered and coughed its way along for the last few miles. With God's help, they arrived at the Gold Mines safely

A man who lived at the settlement was expecting Wesley and welcomed the two men into his simple house. After an evening meal, Chico and Wesley decided to bring the outboard motor into the house to dry it out in time for our return trip. Chico poured the petrol out of the motor into an open can while Wesley held a Tilly Lamp to throw light on the operation. Suddenly, there was a burst of flames as the petrol fumes ignited. Everyone in the house screamed and ran for the door and into the street, except for the man of the house. First, he ran into his bedroom and grabbed a suitcase to carry it outside. People who live in these simple forest homes keep their money and other valuables they may possess in a locked suitcase.

Wesley managed to drag the outboard motor outside the house into the night air. He then saw flames licking around the bottom of two petrol cans on the wooden floor. Knowing that the cans would probably catch fire, he caught the already hot handles of both cans and dragged them outside. Wesley escaped serious injury when the cans exploded and threw flames into the air.

By this time many people came with pots and tins of water to help put the fire out. Sadly, everything inside the house was destroyed. Wesley felt bad and very embarrassed about the incident. He was also touched by the man's reaction. Even though the owner was not a Christian, he had shown goodwill in giving the missionaries hospitality. Wesley made an attempt to recompense the man for his loss as best he could.

Without fuel, the two men had to make their return trip to Altamira by paddling the canoe upstream. Progress was slow as they edged their way against the strong current by hugging close to the riverbank to avoid the main flow. They were very glad when they rounded another bend on the river and finally saw Altamira just as the sun was setting. It had been a hard and eventful trip, but they rejoiced they had been able to implant the precious seed of the Word of God in the hearts of the people at the gold mines.

Numerous wood-burning launches travelled from Altamira for hundreds of miles to the upper Xingu collecting rubber latex and Brazil nuts as they went. Sometimes Wesley travelled on these vessels, and when he did, each evening he conducted a Gospel witness for the passengers and people who lived at wherever the launch stopped to take on firewood. The food on board was always the usual rice, beans and farinha. Drinking water came straight from the river without being filtered. With hygiene being virtually zero, Wesley and the other passengers were vulnerable to picking up intestinal infections. After a few days on one of these trips, he became ill with amoebic dysentery. He had planned to travel up the River Fresco to a Kayapo village evangelising as he went. However, this tummy bug made him have a change of plans.

When the boat got to São Felix, a village at the mouth of the River Fresco, he could go no farther. Due to the constant and severe pains in his stomach, he decided to stay in the village while the boat continued up the River Fresco. A kind and elderly lady offered a room to Wesley in her humble riverside home. She cared for him while he waited several days for the boat to return.

In spite of this lady's attention, Wesley continued to feel weak. He was suffering so much pain he was sure he was going to die. He called upon God, and as he did he knew that friends and supporters back home would be praying for him without knowing his plight. God answered their prayers and his.

Out of the blue, a man arrived who just happened to have some medicine for dysentery. Wesley gladly took what was offered to him, and in a few days, he improved. By the time the boat arrived back from its trip up the Fresco Wesley was feeling a lot better and well enough to travel to Altamira.

When he arrived back in town, the believers could scarcely recognize Wesley since he had lost about seven kilos weight.

After eighteen months in Altamira where Wesley made many friends and enjoyed fellowship with the believers, he turned his thoughts to travelling home for his first furlough. During that first term in Brazil, he had faced many situations and proved the Lord's grace time and again. One thing he was persuaded of was that he would not return to Brazil as a single man.

Wesley knew he needed a wife.

CHAPTER 8

Winifred and Wedding

THE LONG BOAT journey from Brazil to Liverpool gave Wesley plenty of time to think about his future. He still remembered his first encounter with Winifred Dundas at Lisburn Road Methodist Church, but he had lost touch with her. While in Brazil communication with family and friends in Ireland and elsewhere had been extremely difficult. It generally took letters up to a month to arrive in Brazil, if they did arrive. Mail often went astray, but to who knows where? Furthermore, there were no Post Offices in Santa Inez or Altamira. Wesley had to depend on someone bringing mail from Belém by hand or to travel to the State capital to pick it up.

These difficulties added to Wesley losing contact with Winifred. During his voyage home, he wondered what she was doing. The last he knew was that she had gone to Dublin for her nursing training. He not only thought about Winifred, he prayed that the Lord would show him – and her, the right way forward. *Would she be interested in marrying me? Would she be prepared to live in Brazil? Would the Mission accept her?*

These thoughts constantly turned over in Wesley's mind as the ship cut its way across the Atlantic. He was content to leave it all in the Lord's hands, although he also believed in faith and works. He, therefore, decided he would do something about it.

Much had changed in Britain since Wesley had left for Brazil just over four years earlier. King George VI had died and a young new Queen occupied the British throne, H R H Queen Elizabeth II. Britain's great wartime Premier, Sir Winston Churchill, had returned to be Prime Minister. These changes were of national importance, but Wesley Gould had other matters to think of.

He was glad to meet his family in Portadown where he enjoyed some of his favourite Irish foods that he had missed, and he renewed fellowship with those who had supported him while he was away. Joe Wright, a former missionary in Brazil for many years with UFM and brother of martyred missionary, Fred Wright, was Irish Secretary for the mission. Joe was glad to see Wesley and keen to enlist his help for deputation tours all over Ireland. Wesley was happy to co-operate in all this, but he was anxious to make contact with Winifred.

Winifred Hannah Dundas was born at Tabagh, a short distance from Enniskillen in County Fermanagh. She was the fifth of seven daughters and also had two brothers. During Winnie's birth, Mrs Dundas was in some difficulty when a neighbour, although unqualified, stepped in to deliver the new baby girl. Mr and Mrs Dundas were so overjoyed with the safe arrival of another little daughter that named her after the neighbour, Winifred. Mrs Dundas also felt that God had spared their little daughter for a special purpose.

The Dundas children had the blessing and privilege of Christian parents. Their dad was Sunday School superintendent at Derrygonnelly Methodist Church and a popular local preacher in the Methodist circuit.

After her primary education at Derrygonnelly Primary School Winnie went on to the Model School in Enniskillen. Sunday was always a special day in the Dundas home. The children seldom ever missed their Sunday School classes, and attendance at church was a regular feature of their weekly routine. Added to this, Mr and Mrs Dundas prayed for and with each of their children and taught them the Scriptures. For all of this, the Dundas children knew that religion and church-going were not enough to become Christians and have the assurance of salvation.

Winnie was a young teenager when she trusted Jesus Christ as Saviour at an Irish Evangelistic Band mission conducted in a portable hall by Frank Marshall and Billy McClintock. Her conversion did not manifest a big outward change in Winnie's life, for she had never been addicted to bad habits or behaviour. The change was in her heart. She knew that her life, body, soul and spirit belonged to God, purchased by the Saviour's blood, and she wanted to serve God as a missionary.

This desire to be a missionary seemed to be influenced by Winnie's mother who always said she would love to have been a missionary. Winnie remembers her mother writing out Bible verses on pieces of paper, placing them at conspicuous places in the kitchen and then endeavouring to memorise them while she baked or washed dishes. She also encouraged Winnie to commit these Bible texts to memory and taught her to lean on God's promise in Proverbs 3:5, 6, "Trust in the Lord with all thine heart; and lean not unto thine own understanding. In all thy ways acknowledge him, and he shall direct thy paths."

Winnie's aim was to be a missionary nurse. However, there were several steps to be taken before the door to nursing opened. After finishing her schooling in Enniskillen employment at a local Post Office opened the way for her to secure a civil service job at the government building at Stormont in Belfast. That was a big move for a country girl like Winnie. It meant she had to leave home and move into lodgings in Belfast where she did not know anyone. However, this resilient girl made good use of her time by pursuing further education at the Belfast Technical College, all with the view of becoming a nurse.

In the course of her employment at Stormont Winnie was transferred to the Ministry of Agriculture offices in Balmoral Avenue. This turned to be a major piece of the jigsaw of God's providence in her life, for while there she attended Lisburn Road Methodist church where she was introduced to a Bible College student named Wesley Gould.

Winnie's attendance at the Bible Study classes at Belfast Bible School helped her get to know Wesley and several other students. Their single-mindedness and dedication stimulated Winnie to take steps that would open the door for nursing. Further to this desire to serve her Saviour, Winnie felt God calling her to Brazil after attending a missionary rally at Wellington Hall Belfast. Willie McComb, veteran missionary and founder of the Acre Gospel Mission, gave a challenging account of his experiences in the Amazon. The Saviour had said, "Behold I have set before thee an open door that no man can shut." Little by little and in due time that door would open for Winnie.

Wesley was at the Missionary School of Medicine in London when Winnie enrolled for her nursing training at the Adelaide Hospital in Dublin. Again she was in unfamiliar surroundings but quickly made friends with other nurses, several of whom were Christians. Her involvement with them introduced her to the Nurses' Christian Fellowship. She eventually became secretary of this group.

While she was in Dublin news came through that her dad had fallen from a horse. From that, he developed influenza meningitis and after a short time, he died. He was only fifty-nine years old. His dedication and example made a big imprint on Winnie's life and spurred her on to do and be the best for her Saviour.

After four years in Dublin Winnie began her midwifery training at the Royal Maternity Hospital in Belfast. It was while she was there that Wesley Gould arrived home from Brazil on his first furlough. Since she last saw him in 1948 there had been little contact. This was largely due to the limited means of communication at that time. Winnie was therefore very surprised when she received a phone call from Wesley asking to meet with her.

Wesley travelled to Belfast on a fine summer evening for his first date with Winnie. They walked from the city centre to Belfast's Botanic Gardens, exchanging their news all the way as they went. Both of them knew this was for real.

In the idyllic and appropriate setting in front of the beautiful Palm House, Wesley popped the question and asked Winnie to be his wife and go back to Brazil with him. He had no ring to place on her finger at that moment and knew that he would have to seek permission from

Winnie's mother, but he was anxious to have Winnie's response. He was overjoyed when it was an affirmative "Yes!"

Permission from Mrs Dundas was readily granted even though two of her other daughters, Cherrie and Edith, were planning to get married that same year. Wesley and Winnie met up again in Belfast to buy the engagement ring. Wesley and Winnie always remember that the ring cost the equivalent of a month's missionary allowance.

While their wedding plans were developing Winnie had to apply to UFM for acceptance, and Wesley had to gain permission from the mission to get married. To be better equipped for missionary life Winnie enrolled for a short course at Belfast Bible College which by this time had moved to Thronemount on Belfast's Antrim Road.

The 8th July 1953 was a lovely summer day when Wesley and Winnie tied the knot. The venue for the big day was in Enniskillen and appropriately named Darling Street Methodist Church. It was a real missionary occasion. Wesley's former colleague at Belfast Bible School, Billy McIlfatrick, was on missionary furlough from India. He stood at Wesley's side as best man. Priscilla Irvine, Winnie's nursing friend and WEC missionary to Ghana, was the bridesmaid. Family and friends were there to join in the happiness of the great day as these two lives were united to serve their Lord.

After their honeymoon in Portrush, on Northern Ireland's north coast, Wesley and Winnie returned to County Armagh. While Winnie worked for a few months at Lurgan Hospital Wesley continued in his deputation work with meetings all over the countryside.

In December 1953, six months after their wedding, the new Mr and Mrs Wesley Gould were ready to travel to Brazil. This was Coronation Year for the young Queen Elizabeth II and a whole new adventure for Winnie Gould.

CHAPTER 9

Where is Piracuruca?

WINNIE HAD NEVER travelled so far from home, and when she embarked with Wesley on the Booth Line cargo ship in Liverpool, her excitement was mingled with a little apprehension. The voyage from Liverpool to Brazil took them through the highs and lows of three weeks on the ocean waves. Wesley had made this voyage before, and he had great pleasure in showing his wife around Lisbon, Funchal in Madeira, Bridgetown in Barbados and Port of Spain in Trinidad before they finally arrived in Brazil. During the days at sea, Wesley tried to teach his wife some Portuguese, preparing her for what lay ahead.

In contrast to the first time Wesley arrived in Brazil, he not only had his wife at his side, but he also had brought a little more baggage than before. However, their baggage could not be fully unpacked until they would finally settle in the place they were going to work. Before going anywhere, however, Winnie had to enrol at the language school at the new UFM base at Avenida Independencia in Belém. Soon she was grappling with new phonetics, learning the conjugations of multiple verbs and trying to decipher between masculine and feminine nouns. Winnie was the only British missionary candidate among the ten language students who started the course, most of whom were Americans and Canadians.

While Winnie was studying Portuguese Wesley engaged in colportage evangelistic work visiting various districts of Belém on bicycle and nearby settlements on the River Amazon by canoe. In the evenings he helped Winnie with her language studies. After nine months the language course concluded, and Winnie had gained a good proficiency in Portuguese. She was just glad to have survived the course. Of the ten candidates who started with her, only three finished. Seven of the other new missionaries had become ill or encountered other problems and consequently had returned to their homelands.

During the nine months in Belém Wesley and Winnie had been praying about their future field of service and speaking to the Field Council about the neediest areas in Brazil. The council members suggested that the Goulds should consider pioneering a church-planting ministry in the town of Piracuruca in the State of Piauí in Brazil's impoverished Northeast region.

Piracuruca, an indigenous name that means the "fish that snores", was founded and settled by Jesuits and priests of the Carmelite Order. When Brazil was discovered and colonised by the Portuguese the Jesuits took an upper hand and always left their mark of fanaticism and persecution wherever they went. Brazil is the largest Roman Catholic country in the world, and Piauí was the heartland of Catholic fanaticism and intolerance at that time.

The town is located on the banks of the River Piracuruca, and the Church of Our Lady of Monte do Carmo dominates the town as a lasting legacy of those early religionists.

The economy of the region is largely based on cattle ranching and the extraction of *carnauba*, a native palm tree that produces vegetable resins that are widely used in industrial products such as car wax. For that reason, the largely sandy savannah topography is liberally covered with these carnauba palm trees. The climate is extremely hot, often exceeding 40° Celsius. Besides the extreme and dry heat, rainfall is infrequent, and much to the annoyance of local farmers, the region often experiences up to two years of drought.

Wesley and Winnie flew to Parnaiba, Piauí's second largest city. From there they travelled for eighty miles by rail and bus to finally arrive in Piracuruca where they became the first evangelical missionaries to bring the light of the Gospel to that town. Although they arrived with trust in God and hopes to plant an evangelical church, they soon knew they were in for a spiritual battle.

No welcome mat was rolled out for Wesley and Winnie on their arrival in Piracuruca. Right from the outset the town's two Brazilian priests, Frei Benedito and Frei Chemendes, opposed anyone who spoke of a Bible or presented anything other than Catholicism. They were totally intolerant of the new missionaries in town. This became obvious when the new arrivals tried to rent a residential property in the town. No one would let them have a place because the priests had threatened them with the curse of "Our Lady" if they dared rent property to these "Protestant heretics".

Wesley and Winnie employed the only means they knew to counter such hostility and spiritual opposition; they prayed and asked friends at home to pray with them for an open door in Piracuruca. In a short while, God answered prayer in a wonderful way. Senhor Dodo, a Mason and the town's Notary Public, was leaving Piracuruca to move to another place. He was not a religious man and cared nothing about the priests. He decided to rent his big house right in the centre of town to Wesley and Winnie. The missionaries rejoiced in this development, but the two priests were furious, for they could do nothing about it.

This was Winnie's first experience of living in the interior, and she had to quickly get used to contending with multiple cockroaches in the house and the nocturnal chorus of noisy frogs at the back of the house which overlooked the river. Worst of all were the hundreds of bats that emerged from the rafters every evening. They were not only like swooping Spitfires overhead, they stank, and every day Winnie had to brush up their droppings. Added to this were swarms of bugs and pests that made life quite uncomfortable.

After taking possession of the property and arranging their living quarters, Wesley turned the largest room in the house into a little mission hall. The couple then began to invite the local people to the meetings. This was the next big spiritual battle the Goulds encountered. No one would dare venture through the door of their property, which was only fifty yards away from the Catholic Church on the opposite corner of the town's main square. The priests had been very successful by instilling great fear and intense prejudice in the people's hearts.

Wesley and Winnie decided that if the people of Piracuruca would not come to their house, then they would go to the people. Armed with their Gospel literature and a Tilley Lamp, the two missionaries set out to conduct open-air meetings all over town. There were no Christians to stand with them as yet. When the two forlorn missionaries arrived at a street corner, they began to sing Gospel songs and preach from an open Bible. By their own admission, Wesley and Winnie are not great singers, and they blush at what their renditions of poor singing and broken Portuguese must have sounded like. Nevertheless, they were in Piracuruca as ambassadors for Christ.

When not out preaching the gospel Wesley and Winnie tried to offer practical help to the local people. The only medical help in town was when a local medical student attended the sick when he came home for a visit. In his absence, Winnie treated many sick people and put her midwifery skills to good use. When people found out that she was a qualified midwife they called on her at all hours of the day and night to attend to their wives or daughters.

On one occasion, some people arrived late one day from Brasileira, a village more than forty kilometres away, to ask Winnie for urgent help. A lady was due to have her baby and they feared there might be some complications. The only means of transport for Wesley and Winnie to Brasileira was on a railway trolley, hand-operated by two men pushing levers up and down. They were cautioned to be careful of jaguars coming out of the forest to drink in a stream at night, as they often did.

Thankfully, the journey was uneventful and without any danger. Furthermore, Winnie's aid was greatly appreciated by the family when a baby was safely born.

Wesley also did some dentistry and thereby relieved some people from their toothaches. These gestures were appreciated and enabled

CHAPTER 9 – WHERE IS PIRACURUCA?

them to build some local friendships, but even then these friends were hesitant to attend any sort of evangelical meeting.

Wherever the missionaries went the two priests, with their long black robes fluttering around them, followed after with haste and determination. They inevitably arrived on the scene with a mob behind them to disrupt the open-air meetings. They incited the crowd to create such a racket as to drown out Wesley's voice. The priests also retrieved any Gospel literature the missionaries might have distributed and on several occasions, they had a public bonfire to burn Bibles, Gospel booklets and leaflets. Such was the hostility to the Gospel.

The large family next door to Wesley and Winnie were fanatical members of the Roman Catholic Church. The mother had given birth to twenty-one children, one of which had died in a drowning accident. She reared her remaining twenty sons and daughters as faithful Catholics. During this antagonistic time, the mother always got a couple of her children to spy on the missionaries. They would follow Wesley and Winnie around the town to see where they would be holding another open-air meeting. From there the children then ran to inform the priests and give directions to where the missionaries had gone. Very soon afterwards the priests arrived to disperse anyone who might be standing nearby. On the arrival of these fanatical clerics, the people often ran away for fear of them. Anyone who had the courage to stay was confronted by the priests who asked if they were Catholics. If the answer were "Yes," as it often was, the priests would say, "Well, my child, this is not the place for you. Come along with me." He took them to a house nearby to make them chant "Ave Maria" until the missionary couple finally moved away.

Through all this persecution Wesley was mindful of Paul's missionary exhortation to Timothy to "endure hardness, as a good soldier of Jesus Christ ... Preach the word; be instant in season, out of season."

It certainly seemed that preaching God's Word was out of season in Piracuruca, but Wesley and Winnie continued steadfastly with their work and witness week after week, and God honoured His Word. Dona Francisca had never seen a Bible before until she received a copy of the Scriptures after she trusted the Lord at the meetings in Piracuruca. Her new-found faith in Christ gave her a great desire to read God's Word. However, her husband did not allow her to open a Bible in their home. To avoid any more domestic rows and be able to read the Scriptures, she sat outdoors at the rear of their home. Even then her husband objected to her having a Bible. The situation became so acrimonious that she had to leave her home. The angry husband demanded that their children make a decision to either follow her and her Bible or to remain with him. The frightened children clung to their mother and went with her to her sister's house. Dona Francisca remained constant in her faith and saw her children trust in the Lord also. Being the first convert in Piracuruca, Dona Francisca is looked upon as the mother of the church.

CHAPTER 10

Keep Going

WESLEY WAS CONFIDENT that Satan had no weapon in his armoury or implement from hell that could withstand the preaching of the Gospel. Light is always greater than darkness, heaven always stronger than hell, and Gospel truth will ultimately dispel the ignorance of men. With this assured conviction, Wesley and Winnie believed that God would cause the glorious light of the Gospel to shine in on those who had been blinded by the god of this world.

In spite of their faith and the constant prayerful support of many friends, there was little response to their work. For the first two years, this pioneer outreach to Piracuruca was very discouraging. There were many times when they felt like shaking the dust off their feet to go to another place where the people might listen and respond to the Gospel. At the same time, in their hearts they had no liberty to pack up and leave. For them, that would be admitting defeat and giving place to the devil. God gave them the grace to persevere.

Little by little, through Winnie's medical and Wesley's dental extractions and other practical help, they were able to gradually break down the opposition of the people. They began to venture into the meetings, and eventually, some of them were converted to Christ.

One night Winnie was called to an accident that had happened just outside Piracuruca. A lorry loaded with bags of rice had many people sitting on the top when it turned over. The nearest hospital was more than eighty kilometres away and there was no telephone communication.Winnie did what she could for the wounded until a doctor arrived. After that many of the injured were transported away for further treatment.

Because they did not have their own transport while in Piracuruca it was difficult for Wesley and Winnie to travel to neighbouring villages to preach the Gospel. Besides not having their own transport they encountered other difficulties when they tried to go to São José, a village fifteen miles away from Piracuruca. When they tried to pay for a ride on a jeep or a lorry they came up against more prejudice. Wesley had heard that the people in São José were fanatical in their Catholicism and that the headman of the village, Senhor Devino, was a very close friend of the two priests in Piracuruca. Furthermore, Senhor Devino owned the only lorry that transported passengers to and from São José.

When Wesley and Winnie decided to go to São José for a few days and have meetings in that village, they were totally unaware that there might be any problems. On the day to travel they loaded their baggage onto the lorry. When Senhor Devino arrived and saw the missionary couple he immediately told Wesley that his friend, the priest, had requested him not to provide transport to São José for the missionaries. Even though Wesley tried to reason with Senhor Devino, the man was not for budging. A crowd of curious onlookers stood by and watched as Wesley unloaded his baggage from the lorry.

The missionary couple assured Senhor Devino that even though he was not willing to take them, they would find other transport to the village. Wesley knew that Devino, even though he had material means and carried some authority locally, was treading on dangerous ground when he opposed the work of God. He was, therefore, not surprised when Devino was killed a month later when he was knocked down by a bus.

Not to be deterred, Wesley hired a jeep to take them to São José that same day they had been refused a place on the lorry. When they got to the village they could not find a place to stay. Senhor Devino had arrived before them and warned the people that a missionary couple would probably be coming. He instructed them not to give these foreigners any hospitality in their homes.

When Wesley and Winnie arrived in São José they realised they were up against a brick wall. They enquired if there was anyone who would give them a place to sling their hammocks for that night. No one offered them anything. Like Mary and Joseph in the Christmas story, there was no room for them in any house. At the same time, they were not turning back and told the local people that if they could not find a house to sleep in that night then they would sling their hammocks in the surrounding forest. They were determined to stay no matter what happened.

Late in the day a very poor lady came forward and offered them a place in her house to sleep that night. Winnie recognised that she had met this woman before. It then dawned on Winnie that she had saved the lady's life a few weeks earlier when the woman got into some difficulties at childbirth. Winnie recalled that on that night in Piracuruca she got a call to help deliver a baby from a woman who was in labour. This turned out to be the same lady, and she was known to be a prostitute

When the woman perceived that Winnie had recognized her she spoke up, "You saved my life so you can come to stay in my house."

Staying overnight in a prostitute's house was not the wisest thing to do so Wesley made an excuse that the woman's house was a bit too far from the village and they wanted a place more central. The poor but grateful woman then spoke to an elderly friend who lived in the village and persuaded her to let Wesley and Winnie stay in her house. Now that they had settled the matter of accommodation, Wesley and Winnie set off for an open-air meeting at a street corner. The meeting followed the same pattern as those they had conducted so often in Piracuruca with both of them singing and Wesley preaching. They were well pleased when a good number gathered around to watch and listen even though it might have been out of curiosity more than anything else.

After the meeting, they distributed Gospel literature before returning to the old woman's house to retire. They had just got into their hammocks when they heard the church bells ringing loudly, firecrackers banging in the air and great excitement on the street. They soon learned that the younger of the two priests had arrived from Piracuruca. The cleric had heard that Wesley and Winnie had defied his attempts to keep them from going to São José. He was so furious that he decided to hastily travel to the village to try to stop the missionaries from preaching the Gospel to the people.

During the next three days, Wesley and Winnie had to contend with this fanatical and half-drunk priest. His constant defaming and insulting behaviour toward God's servants was taken more seriously because he always carried a revolver under his long brown robes. This made him a very dangerous man to deal with.

In spite of the constant insults and dangerous threats, Wesley and Winnie continued to have their open-air meetings each night. At every meeting, the local priest arrived with a procession of people carrying an elevated image of the Virgin Mary. The priest then whipped up the crowd into a frenzy of singing, chanting and shouting in an attempt to drown out Wesley's voice.

During that first visit to São José Wesley felt that they did not accomplish much. However, the news of Senhor Devino's tragic death had a sobering effect on the people. They knew that he had been openly and loudly opposed to the Gospel and the missionaries. After his death, Wesley and Winnie found the people were more open to the Gospel, and soon a few people in the village became Christians.

Wesley had read in Isaiah 54:17, "No weapon that is formed against thee shall prosper." Satan had tried in many subtle and threatening ways to hinder and stop the progress of the Gospel in Piracuruca.

Notwithstanding all the satanic obstacles and opposition, Wesley proved that a Christian worker's weapons are mighty through God to the pulling down of what once seemed to be impregnable strongholds.

CHAPTER 11

Progress with Persecution

L ITTLE BY LITTLE, the barriers of prejudice were being broken down in Piracuruca, and people began to have the courage to attend the evangelistic meetings in the hall. The Word of God, written and preached, did its own work, and local people trusted Christ as Saviour. Sunday School attracted some children, and then adults soon followed. First among the early converts were Senhor Antonio Lima and his wife Francisca. These were the first fruits of the work in the town and the beginning of planting the first evangelical church in Piracuruca. From time to time ministerial students would come to help them, but for Wesley and Winnie, it was a lonely and uphill battle all the way.

Communication to family and friends at home was not reliable. Letters to home took several weeks to arrive, and those coming from Northern Ireland often were not even delivered. Mr Gould, Wesley's dad, went to be with his Lord while he and Winnie were in Piracuruca. Wesley fondly remembered his dad's zeal for the Lord and for his family. He had frequently urged Wesley to forget about Brazil with its difficulties and sacrifices and go into the Methodist ministry at home. He even promised to pay the fees for Wesley to study at Cliff College if he decided for the Methodist ministry. Although he greatly respected his father, Wesley had no such calling and felt his place was exactly where he was: serving God in Piracuruca.

Wesley's mother was also keen for him to enter the Methodist ministry. She even spoke with Winnie to influence Wesley to not go back to Brazil so that he could become a Methodist minister. To this Winnie answered, "Mrs Gould, if Wesley stays, I am going on back to

Brazil without him." That was the end of the family trying to divert Wesley from his calling to Brazil.

While they were facing their arduous work in Piracuruca Winnie learned of her brother's death. Because of the intermittent nature of the postal service, Winnie received this news in a sporadic way. In fact, she did not even hear that her brother had died until several weeks after it had happened. Even then she was not sure which brother had died, the one in Canada or the farmer in Fermanagh, Northern Ireland. Later she received news that it was her brother at home, but she was not given any details how he had died. One thing they did know for sure was that these loved ones had gone to be with Christ.

In 1958 Wesley and Winnie endeavoured to enter another village with the Gospel. Batalha was about twenty miles from Piracuruca, and similar to São José, it was dominated by the Roman Catholic priest. He even dictated to the local municipal authorities, and they feared him.

By this time Wesley had been able to purchase a station wagon to make these journeys over dusty or muddy roads. Also, a few believers from Piracuruca were able to travel with them for these meetings in Batalha. These believers helped with the singing, and some were able to speak of their own conversion.

The first time they went to Batalha a good number of people gathered in the town square to hear the Gospel. Soon they heard the all-too-familiar chant of "Ave Maria" from a mob of people led by the Catholic priest parading from the Catholic Church towards the open-air meeting. Four men were carrying an image of the town's patron saint while the crowd shouted, "Long live Our Lady!" and "Death to the Protestants."

The hostile crowd kept milling around the meeting for some time undoubtedly hoping that the believers would run off. However, the missionaries and the team stood firm until the crowd finally but slowly returned to the church.

The following week, the group from the evangelical church returned to Batalha for another meeting. The priest and his followers repeated the same opposition, but on this occasion, the crowd was bigger and the people more agitated than the week before. Again, after the crowd eventually dispersed, Wesley and his friends carried on with their meeting.

At the end of that meeting, Wesley gave an invitation for anyone who wanted to accept Jesus Christ as Saviour to step forward. Even Wesley was surprised when four men stepped to the front. All of them had heard the Gospel for the first or second time before accepting the Lord. Wesley reported later that not all four were soundly converted, but one of these continued. Senhor Gonzalo became a firm believer and a deacon in the little church in Batalha. Over the next few years, every member of his family also came to know Jesus Christ as Saviour.

Although there had been concerted opposition to the Gospel in Piracuruca and the neighbouring villages by verbal threats, slanderous insults and public processions, Wesley and Winnie refused to be drawn into any form of retaliation. By helping local people medically and socially they established friendship so that their neighbours recognised that these missionaries were not "foreign or Protestant devils" as had been suggested. Also, in preaching, Wesley majored on Jesus Christ as the only Saviour from sin and His sacrifice at Calvary as all that was necessary for salvation. He refused to verbally attack the Catholic Church or promote any denominational label. God honoured his faithfulness as hearts were opened to the Gospel.

Every convert at Batalha was a trophy of amazing grace and a miracle of God's mercy. José Lucimar Rocha was a sixteen-year-old boy when he paraded at the front of the Catholic procession in Batalha on the night that Frei Chemendes led the threatening mob against Wesley and Winnie's open-air meeting. He was an altar boy and devotee of the Catholic Church. His mother, a member of the Legion of Mary, and other members of her family were also in the procession that night. All of them provocatively swung their Rosary Beads at the missionaries as they passed by the meeting. They did this in their ignorance because the priest had told them that their beads would ward off the Protestant's evil spirit. Wesley and Winnie were surprised when Lucimar appeared at the meeting one evening not long after parading with the priest. He was at the meeting week after week and listened attentively to Wesley as he preached about the Lord Jesus Christ. Very soon Lucimar never missed meetings in Batalha, and it was a happy night when he gave his heart to the Lord.

God soon laid His hand on this young man and called him into Christian ministry. Not long after his conversion, Wesley asked Lucimar what he wanted to become when he left school. The young man had no hesitation in giving his answer, "I want to be a pastor."

Lucimar went to study for three years at the mission's high school in Barra do Corda and then to the UFM Bible Seminary in São Luiz for four years. From there he became the pastor of a large church in Parintins, in Amazonas. He married a lovely Christian girl from that town also. God greatly used Lucimar to lead many people to faith in Jesus Christ.

Today, besides his pastoral ministry, Lucimar is a Christian journalist and broadcaster in Brazil and has travelled widely in other countries. He also is Regional Director for the Northeast Christian Evangelical Churches and is the founder of many Churches in Piauí.

A further blessing for Wesley and Winnie was to see Lucimar's whole family, except for one brother, trust Jesus Christ as Saviour. His father, Senhor Fausto, was a watch and clock repairer by trade. He was always in demand and travelled widely in Piauí doing this work. One evening he was sitting outside a house after his day's work when a drunkard he did not even know lifted a heavy club and hit Senhor Fausto on the back of his head. The unexpected blow killed him.

Senhor Fausto's body was transported back to Batalha for burial, but the priest would not allow him to be buried in the town's cemetery because he had left the Mother church and had become a believer. In that part of Brazil, it was necessary to bury the dead within twenty-four hours. With this urgency, the frustrated family had to bury their father outside the cemetery's walls. When news of this spread around town the people were furious with the priest for what he had done. Senhor Fausto had been a respected member of the community. Even the town's Prefect and other leading men were so disgusted that they demanded from the priest that Senhor Fausto's remains be exhumed and be reburied inside the cemetery. The cleric reluctantly had to comply with the demands of the people. At the reburial, Lucimar took the opportunity to preach the Gospel to an even larger crowd in the Batalha cemetery that day.

Another young man who was part of the Catholic procession in Batalha and a school friend of Lucimar was António Augusto. Lucimar's conversion impacted Antonio so much that he also accepted Jesus Christ as Saviour. His mother, a devout Roman Catholic, was very displeased that her son had left her church. Consequently, although he was only a teenager, his mother put him out of the house. Antonio left Batalha for Terezina where he slept rough during his adolescent years. This young man developed a great desire to read the Scriptures and enrolled in various Bible correspondence courses. He was an intelligent young man and soon learned how to fix typewriters. From there he went on to develop his own business in Terezina where he also conducted Bible studies and helped establish a church.

Reviewing Winnie's first four years in Brazil helped the Goulds see the triumphs of the Gospel in a region where Christ had not been known. Now it was time to travel home to Northern Ireland for furlough. Their UFM colleagues, John and Olive Sessoms, stepped in to continue the work in the Piracuruca during Wesley and Winnie's absence.

Wesley at Santa Inês

Wesley in Altamira, 1951

Wesley and Winnie's prayer card, 1953

*Wesley,
Winnie and
Esther in
1973*

Wesley and Winnie's home and the church in Piracuruca

The church in Piracuruca and pastor's house today

Congregation outside the Piracuruca Church

First meetings in Dom Pedro

Outreach meeting in Dom Pedro

Missionary Teresa de Moraes from Dom Pedro with colleague Carol Sue Derstine

Antonio Augusto from Batalha

Wesley extracting teeth

Pastor Lucimar and Lenir with their son Davi

Day School at Piracuruca

Village church in Centro de Esteven

Church and congregation in Igarapé-Miri

Samuel Paulino, pastor at Piracuruca for 15 years and Francisca Cardoso

Belfast Bible College 1945
Back row, left to right: Wesley Gould, David Ross, Robert Mackey.
Front row, left to right: William McIlfatrick, George Wood, Ian Anderson

Marie and Edmund Norwood

Wesley and Winnie in retirement

Philip and Esther with Timothy and Jayne

CHAPTER 12

Transition

A MISSIONARY FURLOUGH is designed to be restful and refreshing. That is not always the case. Wesley and Winnie were thrilled to meet up with family and friends, become acquainted with new nephews and nieces and meet with their prayer partners and supporters at various meetings. Their deputation work kept them busy, and people were amazed to hear their report of how God had marvelously opened new doors in distant Brazil despite the stern opposition. New friends were made, and new supporters came on board as Winnie and Wesley contemplated their return to Brazil.

The undoubted highlight of that year's furlough was the arrival of Esther, Wesley and Winnie's only daughter, into their home and family. She quickly won the hearts and love of her grannies, aunties and cousins. Those same hearts were broken later in 1959 when Winnie and Wesley said their farewells to return to Brazil for another tour of service. Esther was only nine months old at that time.

Their arrival in Piracuruca was so different from the first time they set foot in the town. Not only did they have their little daughter to introduce, but they were welcomed by their missionary colleagues, the believers in the church and even some of the town's folk who had previously been hostile to them.

During their first term in Piracuruca, their primary mission had been to evangelise the lost and establish a church, a body of believers. How grateful they were that this was being realised. Quite a few people in Piracuruca and Batalha had professed faith in Christ, and they formed the nucleus of these two churches.

In 1961 Wesley and Winnie welcomed Edmund Norwood to Piracuruca. Edmund, also from Northern Ireland and single at that time, had already been in Brazil three years. Following language school, he had moved around various works to gain experience. His arrival in Piracuruca was a great help and encouragement to Wesley and Winnie. While Winnie looked after baby Esther and stayed in the town, Wesley and Edmund travelled together to the various preaching points with the Gospel message.

By this time the earlier hostility and prejudice in the town against the Goulds had greatly diminished. Baby Esther helped as neighbours wanted to make friends with the "little English baby." It was also quite a novelty when Wesley bought a bicycle, the first to arrive in Piracuruca. Children were so sure that Wesley would fall off the two-wheeled contraption that they ran after him to see when it would happen. Wesley is thankful that it never did. This novelty encouraged others to buy bicycles, and very soon the bank manager was riding his around town and others followed suit.

Although the beginnings were small, Wesley felt it was time to replace the use of the large room in their rented property with a proper church building. Having secured a suitable site in Piracuruca, Wesley designed, drew the plans and oversaw the construction work. He employed local people for the work, and in 1963 the new church was inaugurated. The church members enjoyed having their own sanctuary, the first evangelical church building in the town.

One of the best memories of Piracuruca was when young Esther trusted the Lord Jesus as her Saviour at the Sunday School. Pointing souls to Jesus Christ was the reason Wesley and Winnie were in Brazil, and they rejoiced at every conversion. Their joy was overflowing when their six-year-old daughter waited behind after the meeting and asked Christ into her heart.

Wesley's church-planting ministry took another step forward in 1967 when they were invited by the Field Council to conduct a survey along the recently opened Brasilia/ Belém highway and see what doors the Lord might open for them. Edmund and Marie Norwood and their baby son, David, replaced the Goulds in Piracuruca and Batalha. Edmund was already familiar with the area since he had worked there in former years with the Goulds and the Sessoms.

Before embarking on the survey for a new church plant, Wesley and Winnie had to make the hard decision of sending their darling daughter off to Belém to be schooled at the Amazon Valley Academy, the UFM school for missionaries' children. This is probably the hardest experience for missionary parents and their children, especially the initial step. Each family must make their individual choice, either to homeschool, return to the homeland for education or send their children to a school for missionaries' children. No mission can or should make a blanket decision for their missionaries and whatever choice each family takes is the right one for them.

Wesley and Winnie travelled to São Paulo in the south of Brazil to purchase a four-wheel drive Jeep pickup. From there they travelled north to Brasilia, the nation's Federal Capital, on reasonably good asphalted roads. After that, the fun began.

The Belém-Brasília Highway, the BR-010 or the Transbrasiliana Highway, was first opened in the early 1960s. This dirt and gravel road, almost 2000 kilometres long, cuts through four Brazilian States. It was opened up through the primitive forest and with all sorts of bridges across almost five thousand rivers, streams and water-courses.

Wesley and Winnie drove their new vehicle along this road where townships had sprung up. At times they were kicking up clouds of red dust which also coated them. After heavy tropical downpours of rain, the dust was churned into deep mud, which caused the Jeep to slide all over the place as if they were on ice.

As they went, they visited small town after small town, all the while praying for God's guidance, *Lord, which town would you have us enter?* They were not looking for scenery or what amenities might be available. They wanted to know which place would need a Gospel witness most. They discovered that the Presbyterian church of Brazil had the foresight of acquiring good sites for prospective churches in most of the new townships.

When they came to Barra do Corda in Western Maranhão, they saw a sign pointing west to Dom Pedro, over a hundred kilometres to the east. Wesley and Winnie stopped in Barra do Corda and wondered where they should go. After lifting his heart to God Wesley felt they should set off next day to survey Dom Pedro.

During that night it poured heavy rain with the result the road was in an appalling condition. Even with a four-wheel drive, the wheels spun in the mud, and at times they got stuck. Wesley afterwards said it was the worst journey they had ever made. However, they persevered until they finally reached Dom Pedro, splattered with mud and soaked to the skin.

Wesley and Winnie knew a lady in the town and at her home, they were able to have a wash, dry their clothes and stay overnight. The next morning they got to know the town. Both of them agreed that it was like a wild-west town with horses and mules on the streets. They found that the local population of just over 3,000 souls was mostly made up of imports from Ceará. Many of these had fled from severe drought and famine or had arrived in search of work. Quite a few were people who were on the run from vengeance and retaliation because of murders and crimes they had committed in their home states. One thing was sure, most of them had brought their superstitions and fanatical Catholicism with them.

Having taken it all in, Wesley and Winnie concluded that this was the place the Lord would have them serve. They consulted the Mission Council in Belém and readily received their approval to seek to plant an evangelical work in Dom Pedro.

After visiting Esther in Belém Wesley and Winnie moved to Dom Pedro three months after their first survey of the town. Remembering the acrimonious beginnings of the work in Piracuruca they were not sure what awaited them in this new town. They were sure that the Lord was with them and that the message of the Gospel was still the power of God unto salvation.

CHAPTER 13

Cameos of Grace

THE ROMAN CATHOLIC priest in Don Pedro was completely different from those Wesley and Winnie had met in Piauí. He was very friendly, and not long after they arrived in town the priest invited Wesley to his house for dinner, and the invitation was gladly accepted. This cleric never opposed the beginnings of God's work in any way.

With a better atmosphere, it was a lot easier for Wesley to start open-air Gospel meetings in the town. He also hired a small hall for evangelistic services. Winnie used her medical skills to treat the sick and people who came looking for help. People were not afraid to attend the meetings, and very soon a few people trusted the Lord. A few cameos of what God did in the lives of several people will give an overall view of what happened in Dom Pedro through the power of the Gospel

José Monteiro; José was a black man who was a well-known drunkard in Dom Pedro. He lived on a constant diet of *cachaça*, local rum made from sugarcane juice. Nearly everything he earned as a tinsmith was spent on this addiction. That meant that his wife had no food for her family or money for clothes.

One day Wesley and Winnie arrived at the street corner near to Jose's house. Winnie went from door to door offering Gospel leaflets and giving invitations to attend the meetings. José received one of these leaflets from Winnie and began to read the Scriptures. The Word of God convicted him so deeply that he decided to attend the meetings. When he arrived at the hall he spoke with Wesley before the meeting began and said he wanted to accept Jesus Christ as personal Saviour. Even as he spoke Wesley was aware of the telltale smell of alcohol and thought that this was another drunkard who had come to disturb the meeting.

Wesley invited the alcoholic to sit down and wait until the meeting ended. Afterwards, José repeated his desire to become a Christian even though he was a little intoxicated. Wesley spoke to him of the way of salvation and had the man call upon the Lord. From that moment José's life was transformed. His wife could not get over the change in her husband, and as a result, she also trusted Christ as Saviour a short time later. With time José became a lay preacher, a deacon in the church and a Sunday School teacher.

Dona Otília. Throughout the first year, God richly blessed the work, and many people were converted. Near the end of that year, a terrible tragedy befell the church. It all began one night when a group of Christians from a nearby town were travelling to Dom Pedro by lorry for a special meeting at the mission hall. On the way, they were singing Gospel hymns. A lady named Dona Otília heard them singing and was so impressed by their joy and happiness that she enquired who they were and where they were going. She wanted to have whatever was making these Christians so happy.

As a result, Dona Otília made her way to the mission hall that night and heard the Gospel for the first time. The blessings of that night were crowned with Dona Otília trusting Christ and becoming a believer. Winnie was moved when she heard Otília's circumstances. She had had seven children but only one had survived. The other six had died early in life.

After her conversion, Otília began to witness to her daughter, Maria, and son-in-law, José Saraiva. Maria and José also had seven children, and Otília was very happy when the family attended meetings in the mission hall. Within a short time, the daughter and son-in-law waited after the meeting one evening, desiring to become Christians.

Maria showed considerable signs of genuine conversion to Jesus Christ and spiritual growth. Her husband was a different story. Wesley always sensed there was something sinister, even satanic about him when he entered the mission hall. He eventually stopped coming to the meetings although Maria continued to attend with her mother.

The situation deteriorated rapidly. First, José started to make false accusations against his wife, including being unfaithful to him. This led to fighting with her and physically beating her. It became a very unhappy home and greatly upset their children who helplessly watched it all.

One day at lunchtime, Maria sat down at a kitchen table when José arrived home in another fit of furious rage. In front of three of their children, he suddenly and violently attacked his wife in a demonic rage plunging a sharp knife into Maria's chest and stomach eight times. She died almost immediately. José ran out onto the street in an attempt to escape but was not able to. He was arrested and in due time was sentenced to a lengthy jail term at the State Penitentiary in São Luiz.

Consequently, Dona Otília gained the custody of Maria's seven children. Ironically, she inherited seven grandchildren in place of the seven sons and daughters she had lost. During the next years, Otília was able to raise her grandchildren in the biblical paths of righteousness.

Dona Andorlina: This lady lived in Centro de Esteven, a village near Dom Pedro. She was converted at one of the meetings at this preaching point, and soon after, most of her family trusted Christ as Saviour. Andorlina was well known in her community, and her transformed life was a very effective witness amongst her neighbours. One of these was João, a devout Catholic, who was building a small chapel for the priest to use to conduct Mass or Novenas when he visited Centro do Esteven. Through Andorlina's witness and the preaching of the Gospel, João became a believer in Jesus Christ. Instead of handing the small chapel over to the priest he gave it to the missionaries for use as a Gospel Hall.

The small sanctuary became a place of worship and witness for the believers in Centro do Esteven.

Teresa Alcantara de Morais: This is one of the most remarkable conversions in Dom Pedro. It was not unusual for Brazilians to have large families. Teresa was one of fifteen children, and probably for economic reasons, she was sent to live with her Aunt Costa. Although Costa was not a Christian Wesley had given her a Bible. The aunt did not pay much attention to the Bible, but Teresa, now a teenager, took to reading the Scriptures every day. Without the prompting of a missionary, God spoke to the teenage girl, and as a result, she attended the Gospel meeting in Dom Pedro where she trusted Christ as Saviour.

Without any encouragement from her aunt or her family who continued at their Catholic church, Teresa attended Sunday school and the weekly meetings. She loved the Bible studies, and God's Word began to shape her life. Right from the time of her conversion she had always expressed her desire to be a missionary. That early desire became a reality. Dona Andorlina told Teresa about the Mission's Bible Seminary in São Luiz. After she finished her education Teresa went on to study at the Bible Seminary, and after graduation became a national mission with UFM (now Crossworld UFM). For more than forty years Teresa has worked with the mission with her American colleague, Carol Sue Derstine, and at present, they are serving God in the city of Bacabal in Maranhão.

With a constant flow of new converts, the church in Dom Pedro grew. God was saving His people one by one. Inevitably, there were disappointments and setbacks. There always are. One night the Goulds woke up to find their house was flooded. The river that flowed through the centre of town had burst its banks after a prolonged and heavy rainfall, and the whole town was under water.

Because of a lack of local employment, many families had to move elsewhere in pursuit of a livelihood. Their departure often depleted the numbers attending the church. Notwithstanding these difficulties,

Wesley and Winnie were delighted to see another church established in a town where Christ had previously not been known. Within a few years, a place of worship was constructed there and opened in 1971.

In due time the church called a Brazilian pastor, and like the church in Piracuruca, this church also became a member of the Alliance of Evangelical Churches, a national organisation associated with UFM Brazil.

This was another labour of love, and for Wesley and Winnie, they were delighted to know that this labour was not in vain.

CHAPTER 14

On the Road Again

L IFE IN DOM Pedro was not without incident. Besides working to establish the church in the town, Wesley frequently travelled to twelve different preaching points in neighbouring villages. There were no paved roads to these places. By this time Wesley had become used to kicking up dust or sand on the rough tracks or manoeuvring his way through deep troughs of mud in the rainy season. It was not unusual for vehicles to become bogged down in the mud or for the engine to break down.

One night when Wesley and Winnie were returning from a meeting at one of these places he ran out of petrol four miles out of Dom Pedro. Within a short while, a lorry pulled in at the side of the dirt track. At first, Wesley thought the driver was coming to his aid but soon found out that he too had run out of fuel. The lorry driver decided to head to town on foot to purchase some petrol and have someone drive him back again. Wesley decided to take advantage of this and gave the driver money to buy some fuel for his Jeep also,

The lorry driver agreed to Wesley's request and set off for the town. The missionaries sat in his Jeep and waited for his return, calculating it would take about two hours. The minutes passed slowly and eventually passed into more than three hours without any sign of the driver. After midnight they concluded that he was not coming so they bedded down for the night in their jeep. The next morning they discovered that when the driver had gotten to town he had decided to go home and sleep instead of returning to his vehicle that night.

Wesley tells about another journey – the events of which are better told in his own words:

> I was going to visit our daughter, Esther, who was at the UFM boarding school and to attend the Mission's Field Committee meetings in Belém, Pará. From Don Pedro to Belém is the distance of 450 miles, the first 150 of which was a dirt road through the open bush and verdant jungle. The only means of transport was on the back of an old lorry with wooden benches to sit on. We were all day and all night crawling and bumping along before we got to the Brasilia-Belém Highway. There I transferred to a bus that took me to the frontier between the states of Maranhão and Pará where I planned to stay overnight before catching another bus to Belém the following morning.
>
> I had never been so weary and tired in all my life as I was that night. I discovered that there was only one little *pensão* (boarding house) in the village, and this was full except for one room. I was told that I could have it if I would be willing to share with another man. This I gladly agreed to in order to have some place to lay down my weary bones. After I had had something to eat I went to bed early. My unknown roommate had gone out and did not come back until late. He was a cattle rancher who was returning from southern Brazil where he had sold some animals. He had a large bag, and no doubt he had a lot of money in it.
>
> When he returned he lay down and very soon we both went to sleep. In my deep sleep I had a dream in which I saw one of the Christians from Dom Pedro in our room and for some strange reason, I felt I had to put him out. While still sleeping, I got up from my bed and went over

to the stranger in the other bed and caught him with both my hands around his throat. I was literally strangling him. At that stage, I woke up to find the man's eyes were bulging out of his head, and he was trembling from head to foot. The not-so-poor rancher was alarmed and frightened out of his wits. He, no doubt, thought I was trying to kill him to rob him of his bag of money.

All these travelling men are armed with knives and guns for self-protection. He could have easily killed me and had a very good case to justify it as self-defense. I tried to convince him it was just a dream, but he would not believe me.

We both lay down again, but not to sleep. He kept watching me, and I kept watching him, both of us equally afraid of each other. The frightened man sat up on the side of his bed, made the sign of the cross across his body and then began to pray to the Virgin Mary to deliver him from this maniac in the room with him.

It was obvious that neither of us would be able to sleep for the rest of that night. I decided to get up and ask the owner of the guesthouse for another room. I never saw the rancher again.

When I reflected on the incident I shuddered to think what might have happened. I thanked God for His protection and for the assurance that people had been praying for me.

Wesley finally made it to Belém, weary in body, but with a strange story to tell to his daughter and members of the Field Council.

Family mattered a lot to Wesley and Winnie. While they were in Dom Pedro they received the sad news that Wesley's mother had gone to be with Christ on Christmas Day. Of course, because of the poor postal service and lack of telephone communication, it was well over two weeks before they received the news of Mrs Gould's home-call. Wesley thanked God for his godly mother who had influenced his life so much. He knew that she had been ill for some time and that his sister Margaret had been caring for her. She died at Margaret's home.

Winnie and Wesley also greatly missed Esther being at home with them. They only got to see their daughter for a few weeks at Christmas and then during the school's two-month summer holiday. Meanwhile, Esther was enjoying life at the Amazon Valley Academy Boarding School in Belém. Most of the other students were also missionaries' children, and although their parents were undoubtedly missing them, these kids bonded together like a family. Because they lived together for so long they established lifelong friendships.

On another occasion, after Winnie had visited Esther in Belém, both were returning to Piracuruca in a bus when they came on a fatal accident. A Jeep full of passengers had turned over at the side of the road. Winnie was the first on the scene to give help. She soon discovered that a priest was already dead. Several other passengers were trapped beneath the vehicle and were unconscious under the Jeep. The nearest Hospital was seventy kilometres away but they had no means of communication. Winnie and others did what they could but their hearts were broken when another of the passengers died. She was a very good student who had disobeyed her parents and instead of travelling by bus had accepted an offer of a ride on this Jeep.

Winnie and Esther were grateful for God's travelling mercies on those treacherous roads and for the protective prayers of God's people.

In 1972 Esther joined her mum and dad when the Gould family returned to Northern Ireland for another furlough.

CHAPTER 15

Help and Healing

WESLEY AND WINNIE'S decision to return to Brazil in 1973 was not made easily. During their year at home in Fermanagh, their daughter Esther had adjusted to her studies at the local high school. Added to this, she enjoyed being with cousins and friends she had made at school. To take her back to Brazil would mean her returning to boarding school in Belém where the curriculum was more designed for American education.

Having weighed up these matters, prayed about them and spoken with Esther and family, they made the difficult decision to let their daughter stay in Fermanagh while they returned for another term in Brazil. A fine Christian couple, Ken and Emily Stevenson, provided Esther with a good home environment, and at the weekends Esther spent time with Winnie's sisters. Even though it was reassuring to know that their daughter was in a good and secure home, it was still with heavy hearts that Wesley and Winnie said their goodbyes when they left for Brazil. Esther also found it difficult to see her mum and dad go.

On their arrival in Brazil, the Field Council asked Wesley and Winnie to go to Igarapé-Miri, a small riverside town on the lower Amazon River, just over a hundred kilometres west of Belém. Transport between Belém and Igarapé-Miri was either by boat or bus, the latter having to cross a large stretch of river on a barge to complete the journey.

For years the Goulds had been involved in a church-planting ministry in Piauí and Maranhão, but this challenge was different.

There was already an established church in the town which had been handed over to the Alliance of Evangelical Churches, the national organisation associated with UFM Brazil.

Sadly, there had been trouble with several Brazilian pastors that the Alliance of churches had sent to Igarapé-Miri. They had brought disrepute on the Christian witness in the town and caused division in the church. Because of all their experience in church planting, Wesley and Winnie were invited to help heal the divisions in the church and restore the Christian witness in the town.

Igarapé-Miri was an extremely poor town. Most of the houses were built of wood taken from the surrounding forest, and many of the houses were covered over with palm leaves. These houses were elevated on stilts because the level of the river near the estuary of the Amazon rises and falls every day with the ebb and flow of the ocean tide.

The only employment in Igarapé-Miri was in two sawmills where loggers floated large trees down the river to be processed and exported to other parts of Brazil and abroad. The Amazon climate was different from the high but dry heat of Maranhão. The tropical climate was not only very hot, the constant high humidity and regular rainfall made it very sticky. Because of its proximity to the river, fish was plentiful, all sorts of fish, some weighing up to four hundred pounds.

The surrounding forest stretches for thousands of miles and is broken only by multiple waterways, large tributaries and fast flowing streams that flowed like arteries to make the Amazon basin "the lung of the world." The vast expanse is a zoological and botanical paradise where numerous animals, many of them dangerous, roam freely.

It was not uncommon to see some of these animals in town. Many people had beautiful and colourful Macaw birds as pets while others captured and caged the small and sweet-singing Uirapuru for their homes. Wesley was not too keen on providing a home for forest animals, but even then these creatures had a way of invading his house. Bathroom and toilet facilities in these places were basic.

One day when Wesley was having a shower in their improvised bathroom, he was unaware that a small snake had got caught in the narrow drainage pipe. The soapy water coursing down the drain blinded the snake and being unable to turn around, the small snake forced the drain cover open and popped out onto the bathroom floor at Wesley's feet. Small snakes can be very venomous so Wesley made sure that this one would not survive to do any damage. He was glad it was his time for the shower and not Winnie's, or he might have heard a few shrieks and yells at the appearance.

On another occasion, a *mucura*, a large possum, was found hiding in the rafters of the house. Wesley summoned one of the believers to come and shoot it. The shot frightened the animal. It fell to the ground and pretended to be dead. The *macura* sprays a foul-smelling fluid for protection, but a lady from the church completed the job and killed the animal. She then took it home for her family's dinner.

Wesley discovered that the Igarapé-Miri was also a stronghold of spiritism and voodooists. Despite awareness of the evil powers of darkness, he also knew and had proven that the Gospel had dynamic, divine and delivering power to free people from the power of Satan. As he had done before, week by week he preached the Gospel and led studies in God's Word. Winnie's attention to sick people in the town also helped their witness for Christ.

A young man, who had been involved with local spiritists when they held séances in his home, became ill. His concerned but deluded father, hoping for a cure, sent the young man to a famous witch doctor whose practice was more than 100 miles from their home. After he had been gone for three months the lad returned in a worse state than when he left.

A Christian lady from the Evangelical church brought the young man to the church prayer meeting one night. During the time of prayer, the boy let out an unearthly scream and began rolling on the floor. It was obvious he was demon possessed. Wesley and a few believers laid hands on him and commanded in the Name of Jesus that the evil spirit leave him. The young man returned to his seat and remained quiet until the end of the meeting.

About a month later the young man died; the family believed it was as result of whatever the witch doctor had given their son. The father, who also was a spiritist, invited Wesley to conduct the boy's funeral in the family home. Although it was a tragic situation it gave Wesley an opportunity to preach the Gospel to the family and their neighbours.

It was not uncommon for the Catholic people to invite Wesley to conduct a Gospel meeting in their home and for their neighbours. Such was the case with Senhor Augustino. He invited so many that there was barely room for them in the house even though most of them were sitting on the wooden floor. Although this was the first time for Augustino to hear the Gospel, he accepted Jesus Christ as personal Saviour at the end of the meeting.

Another friend who attended Augustino's meeting invited Wesley to conduct a meeting in his house the following week so that he too could become a Christian. Wesley tried to press upon him that he did not have to wait until the next week; he should accept Christ that same night, as next week might be too late. When the man insisted that it be the next Friday night, Wesley suggested that he attend the church meeting on Sunday night and accept Christ then. The man agreed to go with his friend, Senhor Augustino.

Just before the time of the Sunday evening meeting, the heavens opened and another tropical downpour washed through the town, turning the streets into rivers of mud. Normally, when that happened, nobody would venture out to a meeting. They would not want to sit for an hour or more in wet clothes. Wesley and Winnie, therefore, concluded there would be no meeting that night. They were sorry that Augustino and his friend would not be able to be there as they had promised.

Their faith was small. When they opened the church door to look out, there coming down the street, soaked to the skin and wading through mud and water, were Augustino and his friend. Both men were united in Christ that night when the man called on the name of the Lord for salvation.

Hundreds of families lived in riverside dwellings along the shores of the Amazon. Wesley often travelled by small launch at night to these scattered settlements to conduct Gospel meetings. Sometimes the scene seemed idyllic with the reflection of the full moon shimmering on the wide expanse of the Amazon. The people climbed the muddy bank to the simple riverside house, left their paddles at the door and sat on the bamboo floor. Wesley's Tilley Lamp outshone the little oil lamps in the houses but attracted thousands of flying insects, including mosquitoes and other bloodthirsty bugs. Often he preached the Gospel in these rustic and unusual conditions to large crowds of simple forest dwellers.

One such place to which they occasionally travelled in their little launch was about six hours up river from Igarapé Miri. They had many good meetings there, and they had the joy of pointing quite a few to faith in Christ. Wesley will always remember his last time he visited this place:

> Our return journey to Igarapé-Miri depended on the tide. If the tide was out, the small river inlet would be too shallow for our launch to pass, and therefore, we would have to wait until about midnight for the tide to come in before we could begin our journey home.
>
> To make matters worse I took a severe pain in my stomach after the meeting that night. I don't know what could have caused it. I did not eat much of the boiled pork that was provided for our evening meal, but I was in agony and we had no medicines to relieve the pain.
>
> When we finally got on our way, I was still suffering. I tried lying down in a hammock to see if it would help, but it only seemed to make it worse. I found that the only way

to get a little bit of relief was to stand up and hold on to the side of the launch as it chugged along in the darkness. About two o'clock in the morning, the pain suddenly and completely disappeared. It was a moment of unforgettable relief.

The next day I was telling one of the Christians in town about what had happened and he said that he woke up during the night and felt a strong urge to pray for us on our return journey on the launch. It seems it was at that very hour when he was praying that the pain left me. God indeed hears and answers prayer.

While still in Igarapé-Miri their daughter, Esther, arrived from Ireland. Although she had been happy and well cared for in Fermanagh, Esther had missed her mum and dad; she also missed life in Brazil. She, therefore, decided to join her parents in Brazil, much to Winnie and Wesley's delight.

Esther found life in Igarapé-Miri quite primitive, but she also found it adventurous. While she was there many new believers declared their faith in Christ in the waters of baptism. Wesley and Winnie were overjoyed when Esther joined these converts and was baptised by Wesley.

During their time in Igarapé-Miri, the Gospel testimony in the town had been restored, and the church had largely recovered from their earlier problems. The Alliance of Evangelical Churches was able to designate another pastor to take Wesley's place in leading that work.

CHAPTER 16

The Last Round-Up

WHEN EDMUND AND Marie Norwood went home on furlough the UFM Field Council asked Wesley and Winnie to take their place in Teresina, the capital of Maranhão. This was quite a change for the Goulds for they had always worked in the interior regions of Brazil in smaller towns where the pace of life was much slower, and where the people were generally poor and simple.

Terezina was a large and modern city with a population in excess of 300,000. Where Wesley and Winnie had been used to jostling with ox carts, mules and horses or paddling canoes on the river, here in this city they had to contend with all sorts of motorised vehicles on better roads.

During Edmund's time in the city, he had helped the believers build a mud-walled construction as a temporary place for the meetings. Wesley worked alongside these believers to extend the Gospel witness to Buenos Aires, an impoverished district on the outskirts of the city. After the Central Evangelical Church in Terezina bought a mud dwelling house in that district, Wesley and some believers knocked down several inside walls and converted the former residence into a Mission Hall.

With the building ready, Wesley and Winnie visited homes all over Buenos Aires to invite the people to the Gospel meetings, and they invited the children to the Sunday school. The response was encouraging, and soon they were able to have a weekly Sunday school and regular Gospel services every Sunday night. God's blessing was on the preaching of the Gospel week after week, and people were converted to such an extent that the congregation grew more quickly than the mother church in the city.

Just before they left Buenos Aires a sixty-year-old woman who all her life had been a spiritist, was converted. Following her conversion, she suffered a lot of demonic oppression. She was plagued with doubts and fears, and she could not sleep at night. Wesley encouraged the believers at the church to stand with the lady in prayer. God gave her a glorious deliverance, and this testimony was a blessing and encouragement to all the believers. The lady left Terezina to return to her home in south Brazil and went home a different woman.

When their term in Brazil was nearing completion and another furlough was due, Wesley and Winnie were faced with big decisions. Esther, who was with them in Terezina, was now a young adult. She had been very accommodating for her parents throughout her childhood when they sent her to boarding school and moved from place to place. They felt that they needed to provide her with a stable home in Northern Ireland.

Furthermore, Wesley's sister had cared for his mother until she died and now was attending to his brother who was seriously ill. Wesley felt that after thirty years in Brazil, he and Winnie needed to share some responsibility with their families at home. At the same time, they loved Brazil and God's work in that country. Their decision was not taken lightly, but having prayed about it, talked it over with Esther and taken counsel from colleagues, they finally decided to uproot from Brazil and return to Northern Ireland indefinitely.

Before leaving Brazil in 1978 Wesley and Winnie took Esther with them on a farewell tour to visit their friends in Piracuruca, Batalha and Dom Pedro and other places where they had worked over the previous thirty years. They were delighted to renew fellowship with many sons and daughters in their Christian faith.

Senhor Gonzalo, one of the men who waited behind in a meeting in Batalha and accepted Christ, invited the Gould family to his home. Gonzalo, a goat farmer, had become a deacon in Batalha Evangelical

Church. All of his family, except for his mother, had also become Christians. When Wesley and Winnie met the family again they found that the old mother had not yet accepted Christ. Gonzalo was very concerned for his mother, but he took heart believing that God would save her. Senhor Gonzalo embraced Wesley and thanked him for coming to Batalha in spite of all the persecution. "If it had not been for you and Dona Winnie," said Gonzalo, "I would never have known Jesus Christ as my Saviour. Thank you, thank you."

There was a great farewell service in Piracuruca when the church was packed to capacity. There was much reminiscing. Those who were children during Wesley and Winnie's former years in the town were now married, and some of their children attended the Sunday school. Wesley summed up the evening with Psalm 126:6; "He that goeth forth and weepeth, bearing precious seed, shall doubtless come again with rejoicing, bringing his sheaves with him."

These words also summed up Winnie and Wesley's many years of devoted service in Brazil. They "shall doubtless come again with rejoicing, bringing their sheaves with them."

Just like their years of living in Brazil, their departure from the country was not without incident. Wesley had reserved their passages from Recife to London in good time. A week before their trip he went to the travel agent and confirmed that they had all in hand, especially passports and tickets. Afterwards, he and Winnie stopped at a café for a cool drink. When they had finished Wesley reached for his briefcase that he had placed on the ground beside their table. It was gone, passports, tickets and other papers. Thieves had furtively stolen his briefcase from under their noses.

During the next few days and right up to the day of their departure they were in a fluster of activity to have passports and tickets replaced. Thankfully these came through on time, but that was not the last setback. Esther's friend, who lived in Recife, was keen to take Esther to see Recife's colourful celebrations of Brazilian Independence Day, 7th September. While she was away with her friend, Wesley and

Winnie were busy getting all their luggage to the airport, having been assured that the friend would leave Esther there in time for their flight.

Wesley and Winnie got to the airport early. They waited and waited for Esther, but there was no sign of her. Urgent prayers were shot to heaven in the hope that she would arrive soon. When final calls began being made for the flight, Esther finally arrived. The frustrated family rushed through the check-in, and they were the last people to board the plane.

It seemed as though Brazil was reluctant to let them go.

CHAPTER 17

Beyond Imagination

ARRIVING HOME IN Northern Ireland presented as big a culture shock to the Goulds as the first time Wesley and Winnie had arrived in Brazil. They were home, glad to see family and friends, but what were they to do? In a sense they were out of a job, they had no home and very little money. At the same time, they knew that God had guided them, protected them and supplied their needs for years, and they had the same confidence that He would do the same again.

Wesley had retained his membership at Thomas Street Methodist Church in Portadown where he had trained as a local preacher before going to Brazil. The Thomas Street circuit did not have enough supply ministers to meet the need of its seven churches. When the church learned that Wesley was available, he was invited to become the Circuit Evangelist at Thomas Street Methodist. Assured that this was God's open door for him, he accepted the challenge, and this provided Wesley with opportunity for ministry and provided the family with an income.

A Methodist manse was also made available to the missionary family, but it was empty and bereft of all furniture and furnishing. When this came to the attention of George Allen, a local well-known Christian businessman who had supported Wesley and Winnie for many years, he decided to do something. He spoke with his friend, Albert Prentice, another local businessman, about the matter. Albert said that he had a home in the south of England that had just been sold and the Goulds were welcome to have the contents providing they could find transport. George Allen provided the transport and the removal men.

Within a short time, the removal van arrived with everything that was needed to furnish every room in the manse, including, carpets and curtains. It was the Lord's provision.

With the same zeal that characterised Wesley's Christian service in Brazil, Wesley devoted himself to the Lord's work in the greater Portadown circuit and beyond in various Methodist churches.

Esther enrolled for evening classes at Lurgan Technical College and soon found employment in a Portadown pharmacy. On 7th April 1984, Esther married Philip Ryans and they settled nearby in Tandragee. God blessed their home with two children, Timothy and Jayne.

Wesley's tenure at Portadown Methodist Circuit ended when a new minister was appointed to the post. At that time Joe Wright, a former missionary in Brazil and former Irish Secretary of UFM, and Walter Leech, Secretary of the UFM Irish Council, approached Wesley and invited him to fill the vacancy of the Mission's Irish Secretary.

Wesley served for one year as the Irish UFM Secretary after which he retired to their home in Craigavon.

Wesley and Winnie were able to make two return visits to Brazil. In 1991 they visited Piracuruca and Batalha where they were amazed to see the growth of the church and renew fellowship with believers and friendship with townsfolk. They also went to visit Dom Pedro where they were so encouraged to see the fruition of what the Lord had done in that town. They were most encouraged to see so many young believers grow to become stalwarts in the church and many of them serving God in various places.

In 1992 the UFM Field Council invited Wesley and Winnie to be hosts at the mission's base in Belém. Always available to serve God, they accepted the invitation and were there for three months. Sadly during this visit, Winnie suffered badly from erysipelas, an acute infection with a burning and painful rash on her right leg.

Wesley and Winnie have had a long, full and happy life in the Lord's service. They are glad they have lived to see that their labours for Christ were not in vain. Not only was their work not in vain, but God has prospered the work far beyond their imagination, and it is still growing. Theirs has not only been a work of faith, it has been an experience of faith triumphant.

Is this not what God had promised? "Now unto him that is able to do exceeding abundantly above all that we ask or think, according to the power that worketh in us" (Ephesians 3:20).

Those triumphs of faith continue today.

> Where colleges do not exist
> God's precious Word to teach,
> Missionaries do steal inside,
> Thy hungering servants reach,
> In secret, they explain God's Word,
> To pastors, teachers there;
> "Lord, guard their venues, keep them safe,"
> Should be our daily prayer.
>
> Give praise to the Lord,
> Proclaim His name,
> Make known among the nations
> What he has done,
> Sing to Him, sing praise to Him,
> Tell of His wondrous acts,
> Glory to His name,
>
> Winnie Gould

Postscript

ON TWO OCCASIONS, 2014 and 2016, Winnie's niece, Ann Mylam, visited the churches in Piracuruca. She was able to spend time with believers in their homes and help in the churches' teaching programmes. Besides being a great encouragement to the believers, these visits strengthened the bond that Winnie and Wesley continue to maintain with the Brazilian churches. Every week, by the wonder of modern social media, they receive news from pastors, missionaries and many believers and pray for them.

Ann and her husband Barrie are also involved with Brazilian students who are studying English in the United Kingdom.

UFM Worldwide

S INCE ITS INCEPTION in 1931 UFM has always sought to take the Gospel to those who have the least opportunity to hear. This account of Wesley and Winnie Gould's story of how they sought to accomplish this shows the true pioneering and sacrificial spirit that is needed to complete this task. In the beginning UFM missionaries worked in Brazil, DR Congo and Papua New Guinea. Since then UFM missionaries from N Ireland have also served in Bulgaria, France, Ireland, Ivory Coast, Senegal, Sierra Leone, India, Papua, Spain, SE Asia and Uganda and in multimedia and digital technology ministries.

Throughout the province prayer groups continue to meet regularly to pray for our missionaries and their ministries. As this book clearly demonstrates without prayer we can do nothing. Prayer group members are very knowledgeable about the work and our missionaries around the world are conscious of being upheld by the daily prayers of the Lord's people.

A growing work

In recent years, the work of UFM has greatly expanded as the Lord has been raising up a new generation of missionaries. UFM missionaries now work in more than 40 countries around the world and there are many opportunities for missionary service.

It has been very encouraging to receive a steady stream of applications from Christians with a clear sense of call to serve both long-term and short-term in world mission. These new applications make it clear that God is still calling people into strategic mission situations around the world. He is also calling people who are qualified by their training and life and ministry experience to serve in cross-cultural mission.

Major growth areas include the continent of Europe where we now have 58 missionaries serving in 12 countries. Europe is one of the great missionary challenges of our day. It is a post-Christian continent that needs to be re-evangelised. Churches and Christians in Northern Ireland have an open door to travel to all parts of Europe and to seek to reach the more than 500 million people who do not know Christ. One priority is to reach young people, most of whom have had no contact with the Gospel. Our partnership with IFES is focussed on reaching students in Europe.

There are also a growing number of UFM missionaries working amongst Muslim people in 12 different locations. 1 in 6 UFM missionaries now works amongst Muslim people. This is one of the great mission challenges of today. Although some countries are closed to Christians and others severely restrict Christian activities, there are open doors to reach these people. Our digital technology team is providing expertise to assist our own and other missionaries in reaching out to the Muslim world.

God is calling a new generation of Christians into world mission
UFM does not send missionaries but works in partnership with sending churches. It is essential that all Christians applying to UFM, both for short term and long term ministry, have had their call tested and confirmed by their local church. In no sense does the missionary leave the local church to join the mission. We work in full partnership with sending churches from the beginning of the application process and throughout the missionaries' cross-cultural service.

Responding to what the Lord is doing in the life of Christians is a priority for UFM. Applications for missionary service are handled with a high degree of flexibility. This approach has led to UFM missionaries being sent to many new countries and working in a wide variety of ministries. We also work in partnership with national churches and agencies and other mission agencies. It is both encouraging and exciting to see the Lord's purposes for his world being revealed in the growing number of missionaries, countries and ministries.

Committed to the unevangelised

Since 1931, when UFM missionaries took the Gospel to tribal peoples in Brazil, DR Congo, and Papua New Guinea, UFM has retained its commitment to working amongst those with least opportunity to hear the Gospel. Evangelism and church planting remains a priority because of our continuing conviction that so many people around the world are without hope because they are without God. The cross-cultural mission challenges of our day are very great. The work is not complete. People in remote places, and post-Christian societies, need to hear the Gospel. People living in the hard places need to be reached. All that we do is done in fellowship with, and dependence upon, our Lord and Saviour, Jesus Christ, who has all authority in heaven and in earth and whose command to "Go!" we seek to obey.